Extraterrestrial Life

Other Books of Related Interest

Opposing Viewpoints Series
Paranormal Phenomena

At Issue Series
Space Exploration
UFOs

Extraterrestrial Life

Sylvia Engdahl, *Book Editor*

Bruce Glassman, *Vice President*
Bonnie Szumski, *Publisher*
Helen Cothran, *Managing Editor*
David M. Haugen, *Series Editor*

Contemporary Issues
Companion

GREENHAVEN PRESS
An imprint of Thomson Gale, a part of The Thomson Corporation

THOMSON
™
GALE

Detroit • New York • San Francisco • San Diego • New Haven, Conn.
Waterville, Maine • London • Munich

For more information, contact
Greenhaven Press
27500 Drake Rd.
Farmington Hills, MI 48331-3535
Or you can visit our Internet site at http://www.gale.com

LIBRARY OF CONGRESS CATALOGING-IN-PUBLICATION DATA

Extraterrestrial life / Sylvia Engdahl, book editor.
    p. cm. — (Contemporary issues companion)
Includes bibliographical references and index.
ISBN 0-7377-3253-9 (lib. : alk. paper) — ISBN 0-7377-3254-7 (pbk. : alk. paper)
    1. Life on other planets. 2. Human-alien encounters. 3. Interstellar communication. I. Engdahl, Sylvia. II. Series.
QB54.E9456 2006
576.8'39—dc22   2005046228

Printed in the United States of America

CONTENTS

FOREWORD

In the news, on the streets, and in neighborhoods, individuals are confronted with a variety of social problems. Such problems may affect people directly: A young woman may struggle with depression, suspect a friend of having bulimia, or watch a loved one battle cancer. And even the issues that do not directly affect her private life—such as religious cults, domestic violence, or legalized gambling—still impact the larger society in which she lives. Discovering and analyzing the complexities of issues that encompass communal and societal realms as well as the world of personal experience is a valuable educational goal in the modern world.

Effectively addressing social problems requires familiarity with a constantly changing stream of data. Becoming well informed about today's controversies is an intricate process that often involves reading myriad primary and secondary sources, analyzing political debates, weighing various experts' opinions—even listening to first-hand accounts of those directly affected by the issue. For students and general observers, this can be a daunting task because of the sheer volume of information available in books, periodicals, on the evening news, and on the Internet. Researching the consequences of legalized gambling, for example, might entail sifting through congressional testimony on gambling's societal effects, examining private studies on Indian gaming, perusing numerous websites devoted to Internet betting, and reading essays written by lottery winners as well as interviews with recovering compulsive gamblers. Obtaining valuable information can be time-consuming—since it often requires researchers to pore over numerous documents and commentaries before discovering a source relevant to their particular investigation.

Greenhaven's Contemporary Issues Companion series seeks to assist this process of research by providing readers with useful and pertinent information about today's complex issues. Each volume in this anthology series focuses on a topic of current interest, presenting informative and thought-provoking selections written from a wide variety of viewpoints. The readings selected by the editors include such diverse sources as personal accounts and case studies, pertinent factual and statistical articles, and relevant commentaries and overviews. This diversity of sources and views, found in every Contemporary Issues Companion, offers readers a broad perspective in one convenient volume.

In addition, each title in the Contemporary Issues Companion series is designed especially for young adults. The selections included in every volume are chosen for their accessibility and are expertly edited in consideration of both the reading and comprehension levels of the audience. The structure of the anthologies also enhances accessibility. An introductory essay places each issue in context and provides helpful facts such as historical background or current statistics and legislation that pertain to the topic. The chapters that follow organize the material and focus on specific aspects of the book's topic. Every essay is introduced by a brief summary of its main points and biographical information about the author. These summaries aid in comprehension and can also serve to direct readers to material of immediate interest and need. Finally, a comprehensive index allows readers to efficiently scan and locate content.

The Contemporary Issues Companion series is an ideal launching point for research on a particular topic. Each anthology in the series is composed of readings taken from an extensive gamut of resources, including periodicals, newspapers, books, government documents, the publications of private and public organizations, and Internet websites. In these volumes, readers will find factual support suitable for use in reports, debates, speeches, and research papers. The anthologies also facilitate further research, featuring a book and periodical bibliography and a list of organizations to contact for additional information.

A perfect resource for both students and the general reader, Greenhaven's Contemporary Issues Companion series is sure to be a valued source of current, readable information on social problems that interest young adults. It is the editors' hope that readers will find the Contemporary Issues Companion series useful as a starting point to formulate their own opinions about and answers to the complex issues of the present day.

INTRODUCTION

During the past half century, scientists have been actively seeking evidence of extraterrestrial life. The idea that intelligent aliens may exist is not that recent, however, nor did it originate in science fiction. For more than four hundred years, people on Earth have believed that planets of other stars are inhabited.

The late-sixteenth-century Italian philosopher Giordano Bruno was the first author to say that inhabited worlds orbit the stars. At the time, this was a heretical idea because both the accepted theory of physics and religious doctrine held that Earth was the center of the universe. Because of his speculations about other worlds, as well as his disagreement with the Catholic Church on theological issues, Bruno was burned at the stake in 1600.

During the seventeenth and eighteenth centuries, as knowledge of new discoveries in astronomy spread, the belief that all planets in the universe are inhabited spread with it. In fact, from the early eighteenth century until the mid-nineteenth century, this belief was almost universal among educated people. Poets wrote at great length about other worlds. Well-known figures such as Benjamin Franklin and John Adams mentioned them in their writings. In an 1809 sermon, the president of Yale University stated unequivocally that systems of planets were "with the highest reason supposed to exist and to be, like the earth, the residence of intelligent beings, of incalculable numbers, and endless diversities of character."

A Proposal That Humans Are Alone in the Universe

Although in the middle of the nineteenth century it was generally agreed that other planets were home to intelligent beings, this was soon to change. The first well-known scientist to propose that Earth might be the only inhabited planet was William Whewell, a professor at England's Cambridge University. In 1854 he published his book *Of the Plurality of Worlds* anonymously—a common practice at that time—because he felt that it would be improper for someone in his position to become embroiled in a controversy bound to stir up unfavorable publicity. It did indeed arouse a furor. "We scarcely expected," said the *London Daily News*, "that in the middle of the nineteenth century, a serious attempt would have been made to restore the exploded ideas of man's supremacy over all other creatures in the universe; and still less that such an attempt would have been made by any one whose mind was stored with scientific truths. Nevertheless a champion has actually appeared, who boldly dares to combat against all the rational inhabitants of other spheres."

Whewell, whose identity was soon recognized, began his argument by maintaining that science had no real evidence that the planets were inhabited. When a critic protested that he had shown no more than that, he replied: "If, when I have proved that point, men were to cease to talk as if they knew that the planets are inhabited, I should have produced a great effect." He did not leave it there, however, but went on to argue that both science and religion supported the idea that Earth is unique. This led to heated rebuttals, which at times descended to the level of name-calling. Then as now, it was a subject about which people tended to have strong feelings. "There is no subject within the whole range of knowledge so universally interesting as that of a Plurality of Worlds," wrote Whewell's chief opponent Sir David Brewster, an eminent Scottish physicist. "It commands the sympathies, and appeals to the judgment of men of all nations, of all creeds, and of all times."

Those who agreed with Whewell were a small minority; most people continued to believe in the prevalence of intelligent life. But during the latter half of the nineteenth century, there was a gradual shift in thinking. Previously, it had been generally assumed that all planets everywhere—and their inhabitants—were at the same stage of development. During the Whewell/Brewster debate and even earlier, the suggestion that some might be at different stages of cosmic evolution had been made, but this idea did not become common until the 1870s. When it did, people realized that Earth's position in the universe might be no more central in terms of time than in terms of space and that life might not yet have evolved on some planets.

Furthermore, in the late nineteenth century, science began to learn more about the planets of Earth's own solar system. The revelation that these worlds had no breathable atmospheres or visible traces of civilization cast doubt on the prevalent assumption that all worlds had been created by God for habitation. An even more important factor in the decline of belief in intelligent aliens was the assumed impossibility of ever obtaining any information about them. At that time it was felt that science had disclosed so much about the known universe that the limits of knowledge were approaching. No one foresaw that in the twentieth century, new technology for studying the stars would be developed.

New Views of Extraterrestrial Life

Just after the turn of the century, in 1903, another book appeared that challenged the idea of other inhabited worlds. Aptly titled *Man's Place in the Universe*, it was written by the famous British naturalist Alfred Russel Wallace, who was then eighty years old. The magazine *Scientific American*, in an editorial about reactions to the book, noted, "When Dr. Wallace asserts that our earth is the sole abode of life in the universe . . . one school [of thought] claims that he is old and in his dotage; the other, that he has become wise in his old age." Astronomers tended to be in the first group, since evidence did not support Wallace's contention that Earth's solar system was in the center of the universe and that only in the center could conditions be right for intelligent life to evolve. Although they agreed with what he said about the impossibility of life on some worlds, they saw no reason why this ruled out life on every other planet in the vast universe. Biologists, who knew less about astronomy but were more familiar with the conditions needed for life, found Wallace's book more convincing. Furthermore, people attracted to the thought of extraterrestrial life wanted to envision it on the planets of Earth's own solar system; to be told by an expert on organic evolution that it could not exist on neighboring planets such as Mars, on which markings resembling canals had been observed, caused many to become disillusioned about the whole subject.

Gradually, in the early twentieth century, belief in the existence of extraterrestrials declined. The fading hope of finding intelligent life on Mars distracted people from the thought of life elsewhere. Moreover, a then-current scientific theory predicted that solar systems were infrequently formed, and popular astronomy books emphasized how rarely this was thought to happen rather than how many planets might exist in spite of the rarity. So, during a period roughly corresponding to the time between the two World Wars, the idea of other inhabited worlds was out of favor among the majority of those knowledgeable about science—though popular science fiction tales kept the idea alive in the public imagination.

Then, in the 1950s, a revival of belief in intelligent aliens occurred when, for the first time, people began to hope that contact between Earth and extraterrestrials might be possible. Two factors contributed to this hope. The first was the realization that interplanetary travel might be possible. This began with frequent sightings of unidentified flying objects (UFOs); from the late forties on, many people reported that they had seen flying saucers or even visiting aliens. Also, science fiction movies about alien visitors became popular in the fifties, and these movies fueled the speculations of the general public. Then, in 1957 the Soviet Union launched *Sputnik*, the first orbital satellite. The subsequent space race between the Soviets and the United States made space travel a reality and led to conjecture about future travel between solar systems.

The second development of the 1950s that reinvigorated belief in alien life was the development of radio telescopes, which in 1959 led to the proposal that radio signals from distant worlds might be detected. Some astronomers became enthusiastic about this idea and started listening for such signals. The concept gained currency as scientific papers about it proliferated, and by 1972 a report from the U.S. National Academy of Sciences stated, "More and more scientists feel that contact with other civilizations is no longer something beyond our dreams but a natural event in the history of mankind that will perhaps occur in the lifetime of many of us."

Today, however, those who dreamed in the 1970s of receiving radio messages within their lifetime are growing old. At the dawn of the twenty-first century the pendulum is swinging again. Some scientists have been disillusioned by astronomy's failure thus far to detect signals from extraterrestrial civilizations. Furthermore, there have been so many UFO sightings without conclusive evidence of alien presence that even some former believers have begun to feel that the UFO phenomenon cannot be explained so readily. In 2000 the book *Rare Earth* by geologist Peter Ward and astronomer Donald Brownlee again proposed that Earth may be the only inhabited planet, and scientists are becoming more divided on the issue.

Questions for the Twenty-first Century

Discussion of extraterrestrial life today involves at least four separate questions. First of all, is there life beyond Earth? Almost all scientists believe that there probably is. In fact, a search for primitive forms of life on other planets in Earth's own solar system has already begun. But this does not mean they all believe in the existence of intelligent aliens. Complex life, if it exists, is assumed to be far less widespread than primitive life such as microbes.

Second, can science find evidence of extraterrestrial civilizations? Some scientists, mainly astronomers, believe that it can, and they have been searching for such evidence in an effort known as SETI (Search for Extraterrestrial Intelligence). Contrary to a common public misconception, SETI has absolutely nothing to do with UFOs; it is focused exclusively on detecting radio or other signals from planets of distant stars. SETI has so far failed, however, to distinguish any intelligent signals from the noise of space.

Third, have extraterrestrials visited Earth? Many people believe that UFOs are of extraterrestrial origin, but few scientists think so. The statistics that some scientists offer concerning the probable existence of inhabited extrasolar worlds, which are often used as an argument for the reality of UFOs, tell nothing about the ability of aliens to visit Earth. On the other hand, there is no scientific evidence that aliens have not come or could never come. Thus, whether such visitation has occurred remains a matter of personal opinion.

Finally, what would extraterrestrial contact mean to humankind? Many think that hearing from civilizations advanced enough to send information across space, or to come in starships, would be beneficial because it might tell humankind how to solve Earth's problems. Others think that receiving information from them would be harmful because it would destroy humankind's own culture and ability to progress. A few fear that aliens might be hostile. Although these opinions are separate from opinions about the existence of alien civilizations or alien visitation, they often influence them. For example, because people tend to believe what they want to believe, those who feel contact with extraterrestrial civilizations would be beneficial are more apt to expect it will occur soon than are people who feel it would do harm.

Whether or not there actually are any ETs, what people of the twenty-first century think about them is important—it affects opinions about the future and about humankind's place in the universe. As space expert Frank White says in his 1990 book *The SETI Factor*:

> Preparation for contact is well underway within the popular culture. Many of the possible contact scenarios are being played out in books, on television, and in films. These explorations are positive, because they allow people to think about extraterrestrials in a variety of ways. . . . Those who dismiss UFOs as "unreal" might find the phenomenon more understandable if they considered it as another way of getting ready for contact. As with films and television programs, the UFO contacts range from terrifying abductions to calm interactions with kind extraterrestrials who are concerned about our ecological problems and who are humanoid themselves. . . . The people of Earth are planning for contact, some more consciously than others. The trend of interest in extraterrestrial intelligence will continue because it taps into something deep and profound in human nature.

In White's view, "What is at stake in the search for extraterrestrial intelligence is nothing less than our understanding of what it means to be human." The view of Earth from orbit and from the moon, he points out, produced "a realization of the unity and interconnectedness of our planet as a whole system." The search for life elsewhere is bringing about "a realization of the unity and one-ness of everything in the universe. When and if we make contact, we ought to consider how rare and precious life and intelligence are in this vast and ancient cosmos. Within that context, there are no 'aliens,' only 'Us.'"

CHAPTER 1

IS THERE LIFE BEYOND EARTH?

THE LIKELIHOOD OF EXTRATERRESTRIAL LIFE

Neil deGrasse Tyson

Neil deGrasse Tyson is an astrophysicist and director of the Hayden Planetarium at the American Museum of Natural History in New York City. He has written many books and articles about the universe, and has twice been appointed by President George W. Bush to serve on commissions studying the future of America's space program. The following selection is the testimony he gave at a hearing before the Subcommittee on Space and Aeronautics of the U.S. House of Representatives. In it, he comments on public interest in the search for extraterrestrial life and explains the basic concepts underlying the scientific search for it, such as the Copernican principle—the idea that with respect to the universe as a whole, Earth is probably a typical planet rather than a special one.

The discovery of what is now more than seventy planets around stars other than the Sun continues to stimulate tremendous public and media interest. In this case, attention was driven not so much by the discovery of the extrasolar planets themselves, but by the prospect of them hosting intelligent life.

Nearly every space movie to come from Hollywood includes some encounter between humans and alien life forms. Most recently we have the high-budget Mars-based films *Mission to Mars* and *The Red Planet.* The astrophysics appears to be the ladder to what people really care about: whether or not we are alone in the universe. I have empirical evidence to support this contention. If the person next to me on a long airplane flight ever finds out that I am an astrophysicist, nine times out of ten they ask, with wide eyes, about life in the universe. And only later do they ask me about the big bang and black holes. I know of no other discipline that triggers such a consistent and reliable reaction in public sentiment. This phenomenon is not limited to Americans. The time-honored question: "What is our place in the universe" might just be genetically encoded in our species. All known cul-

Neil deGrasse Tyson, testimony before the U.S. House Subcommittee on Space and Aeronautics, Committee on Science, Washington, DC, July 12, 2001.

tures across all of time have attempted to answer that question. Today we ask the same question, but with fewer words: "Are we alone?"

Ordinarily, there is no riskier step that a scientist (or anyone) can take than to make sweeping generalizations from just one example. At the moment, life on Earth is the only known life in the universe, but there are compelling arguments to suggest we are not alone. Indeed, *most* astrophysicists accept a high probability of there being life elsewhere in the universe, if not on other planets or on moons within our own solar system. The numbers are, well, astronomical: If the count of planets in our solar system is not unusual, then there are more planets in the universe than the sum of all sounds and words ever uttered by every human who has ever lived. To declare that Earth must be the only planet in the universe with life would be inexcusably egocentric of us.

The Copernican Principle

Many generations of thinkers, both religious and scientific, have been led astray by anthropocentric assumptions, while others were simply led astray by ignorance. In the absence of dogma and data, history tells us that it's prudent to be guided by the notion that we are not special, which is generally known as the Copernican principle, named for the Polish astronomer Nicholas Copernicus who, in the mid 1500s, put the Sun back in the middle of our solar system where it belongs. In spite of a third-century B.C. account of a sun-centered universe proposed by the Greek philosopher Aristarchus, the Earth-centered universe was by far the most popular view for most of the last 2000 years. Codified by the teachings of Aristotle and Ptolemy and by the preachings of the Roman Catholic Church, people generally accepted Earth as the center of all motion. It was self-evident: the universe not only looked that way, but God surely made it so. The sixteenth-century Italian monk Giordano Bruno suggested publicly that the universe was filled with planets that harbor life. For these thoughts he was burned at the stake. Fortunately, today we live in somewhat more tolerant times.

While there is no guarantee that the Copernican principle will guide us correctly for all scientific discoveries to come, it has humbled our egos with the realization that not only is Earth not in the center of the solar system, but the solar system is not in the center of the Milky Way galaxy, and the Milky Way galaxy is not in the center of the universe. And in case you are one of those people who thinks that the edge may be a special place, then we are not at the edge of anything either.

A wise contemporary posture would be to assume that life on Earth is not immune to the Copernican principle. If so, then how can the appearance or the chemistry of life on Earth provide clues to what life might be like elsewhere in the universe?

The Diversity of Life on Earth

I do not know whether biologists walk around every day awestruck by the diversity of life. I certainly do. On this single planet called Earth, there co-exist (among countless other life forms), algae, beetles, sponges, jellyfish, snakes, condors, and giant sequoias. Imagine these seven living organisms lined up next to each other in size-place. If you didn't know better, you would be hard-pressed to believe that they all came from the same universe, much less the same planet. Try describing a snake to somebody who has never seen one: "You gotta believe me. There is this animal on Earth that 1) can stalk its prey with infrared detectors, 2) swallows whole live animals up to five times bigger than its head, 3) has no arms or legs or any other appendage, yet 4) can slide along level ground at a speed of two feet per second!"

Given the diversity of life on Earth, one might expect a diversity of life exhibited among Hollywood aliens. But I am consistently amazed by the film industry's lack of creativity. With a few notable exceptions such as life forms in *The Blob* (1958) and in *2001: A Space Odyssey* (1968), Hollywood aliens look remarkably humanoid. No matter how ugly (or cute) they are, nearly all of them have two eyes, a nose, a mouth, two ears, a head, a neck, shoulders, arms, hands, fingers, a torso, two legs, two feet—and they can walk. From an anatomical view, these creatures are practically indistinguishable from humans, yet they are supposed to have come from another planet. If anything is certain, it is that life elsewhere in the universe, intelligent or otherwise, will look at least as exotic as some of Earth's own life forms.

The chemical composition of Earth-based life is primarily derived from a select few ingredients. The elements hydrogen, oxygen, and carbon account for over 95% of the atoms in the human body and in all known life. Of the three, the chemical structure of the carbon atom allows it to bond readily and strongly with itself and with many other elements in many different ways, which is how we came to become carbon-based life, and which is why the study molecules that contain carbon is generally known as "organic" chemistry. The study of life elsewhere in the universe is known as exobiology, which is one of the few disciplines that attempts to function with the complete absence of first-hand data.

Is life chemically special? The Copernican principle suggests that it probably isn't. Aliens need not look like us to resemble us in more fundamental ways. Consider that the four most common elements in the universe are hydrogen, helium, carbon, and oxygen. Helium is inert. So the three most abundant, chemically active ingredients in the cosmos are also the top three ingredients in life on Earth. For this reason, you can bet that if life is found on another planet, it will be made of a similar mix of elements. Conversely, if life on Earth were composed primarily of, for example, molybdenum, bismuth, and plutonium, then we would have excellent reason to suspect that we were something special in the universe.

Appealing once again to the Copernican principle, we can assume that the size of an alien organism is not likely to be ridiculously large compared with life as we know it. There are cogent structural reasons why you would not expect to find a life the size of the Empire State Building strutting around a planet. But if we ignore these engineering limitations of biological matter we approach another, more fundamental limit. If we assume that an alien has control of its own appendages, or more generally, if we assume the organism functions coherently as a system, then its size would ultimately be constrained by its ability to send signals within itself at the speed of light—the fastest allowable speed in the universe. For an admittedly extreme example, if an organism were as big as the entire solar system (about ten light-hours across), and if it wanted to scratch its head, then this simple act would take no less than ten hours to accomplish. Sub-slothlike behavior such as this would be evolutionarily self-limiting because the time since the beginning of the universe may be insufficient for the creature to have evolved from smaller forms of life over many generations.

Extraterrestrial Intelligence Must Be Rare

How about intelligence? Since there is still debate on how to define it and measure it in people, I wonder what the question even means when applied to extraterrestrials. Hollywood has tried, but I give them mixed reviews. . . .

Regardless of how Hollywood aliens are portrayed, . . . we must not stand in denial of the public's interest in the subject. Let us assume, for the sake of argument, that humans are the only species in the history of life on Earth to evolve high-level intelligence. (I mean no disrespect to other big-brained mammals. While most of them cannot do astrophysics, my conclusions are not substantially altered if you wish to include them.) If life on Earth offers any measure of life elsewhere in the universe, then intelligence must be rare. By some estimates, there have been more than ten billion species in the history of life on Earth. It follows that among all extraterrestrial life forms we might expect no better than about one in ten billion to be as intelligent as we are, not to mention the odds against the intelligent life having an advanced technology *and* a desire to communicate through the vast distances of interstellar space.

On the chance that such a civilization exists, radio waves would be the communication band of choice because of their ability to traverse the galaxy unimpeded by interstellar gas and dust clouds. But humans on Earth have only understood the electromagnetic spectrum for less than a century. More depressingly put, for most of human history, had aliens tried to send radio signals to earthlings we would have been incapable of receiving them. For all we know, the aliens have already done this and unwittingly concluded that there was no intelligent life on Earth. They would now be looking elsewhere. A more humbling possibility would be if aliens had become aware of the technologically proficient species that now inhabits Earth, yet they had drawn the same conclusion.

The Prerequisites for Life

Our life-on-Earth bias, intelligent or otherwise requires us to hold the existence of liquid water as a prerequisite to life elsewhere. A planet's orbit should not be too close to its host star, otherwise the temperature would be too high and the planet's water content would vaporize. The orbit should not be too far away either, or else the temperature would be too low and the planet's water content would freeze. In other words, conditions on the planet must allow the temperature to stay within the 180 degree (Fahrenheit) range of liquid water. As in the three-bowls-of-food scene in the fairy tale *Goldilocks and the Three Bears*, the temperature has to be just right. . . .

While distance from the host planet is an important factor for the existence of life as we know it, other factors matter too, such as a planet's ability to trap stellar radiation. Venus is a textbook example of this "greenhouse" phenomenon. Visible sunlight that manages to pass through its thick atmosphere of carbon dioxide gets absorbed by Venus's surface and then re-radiated in the infrared part of the spectrum. The infrared, in turn, gets trapped by the atmosphere. The unpleasant consequence is an air temperature that hovers at about 900 degrees Fahrenheit, which is much hotter than we would expect knowing Venus's distance to the Sun. At this temperature, lead would swiftly become molten and a 16-inch pepperoni pizza will cook in nine seconds.

The discovery of simple, unintelligent life forms elsewhere in the universe (or evidence that they once existed) would be far more likely and, for me, only slightly less exciting than the discovery of intelligent life. Two excellent nearby places to look are the dried riverbeds of Mars, where there may be fossil evidence of life from when waters once flowed, and the subsurface oceans that are theorized to exist under the frozen ice layers of Jupiter's moon Europa. Once again, the promise of liquid water defines our targets of search.

Other commonly invoked prerequisites for the evolution of life in the universe involve a planet in a stable, nearly circular orbit around a single star. With binary and multiple star systems, which comprise about half of all "stars" in the galaxy, planet orbits tend to be strongly elongated and chaotic, which induces extreme temperature swings that would undermine the evolution of stable life forms. We also require that there be sufficient time for evolution to run its course. High-mass stars are so short-lived (a few million years) that life on an Earth-like planet in orbit around them would never have a chance to evolve.

The Drake Equation

The set of conditions to support life as we know it are loosely quantified through what is known as the Drake equation, named for the American astronomer Frank Drake (now at the University of California at Santa Cruz). The Drake equation is more accurately viewed as a fertile idea rather than as a rigorous statement of how the physical universe works. It separates the overall probability of finding life in the galaxy into a set of simpler probabilities that correspond to our preconceived notions of the cosmic conditions that are suitable for life. In the end, after you argue with your colleagues about the value of each probability term in the equation, you are left with an estimate for the total number of intelligent, technologically proficient civilizations in the galaxy. Depending on your bias-level, and your knowledge of biology, chemistry, celestial mechanics, and astrophysics, you may use it to estimate from at least one (we humans) up to millions of civilizations in the Milky Way.

If we consider the possibility that we may rank as primitive among the universe's technologically competent life forms—however rare they may be—then the best we can do is keep alert for signals sent by others because it is far more expensive to send rather than receive them. Presumably, an advanced civilization would have easy-access to an abundant source of energy such as its host star. These are the civilizations that would be more likely to send rather than receive. The search for extraterrestrial intelligence (affectionately known by its acronym SETI) has taken many forms. The most advanced effort today uses a cleverly designed electronic detector that monitors, in its latest version, billions of radio channels in search of a signal that might rise above the cosmic noise. The "SETI At Home" screen saver analyzes real data (downloaded from the Internet) for an intelligent signal that rises above the din of cosmic noise. This software has been downloaded by more than 3 million PC users around the world, which actively taps an astonishing level [of] computing power from your plugged-in PC that would otherwise be doing nothing while you went to the bathroom. Indeed, "SETI At Home" is, by far, the largest computational project in the history of the world. I note that these projects in particular received their start-up funds from the Planetary Society, a 100,000-member organization that, among other objectives, promotes the search for life in the universe. Public support for this enterprise is real and it is deep.

The discovery of extraterrestrial intelligence, if and when it happens, will impart a change in human self-perception that may be impossible to anticipate. If we don't soon find life elsewhere, what will matter most is that we had not stopped looking. Our species demands that we keep looking. Deep in our soul of curiosity we are intellectual nomads—in search of other places, in search of other life forms because we derive almost as much fulfillment from the search as we do from the discovery.

COMPLEX LIFE MAY OR MAY NOT BE RARE

NASA Panel Discussion

When the book *Rare Earth* was published in 2000, it aroused a great deal of controversy among astrobiologists. Written by Peter Ward and Donald Brownlee, professors of geology and astronomy respectively at the University of Washington, the book suggests that complex life is rare in the universe and may even be unique to Earth. In 2002 NASA published a five-part debate in its online *Astrobiology Magazine* between Ward, Brownlee, and several other scientists: Frank Drake, a professor of astronomy and SETI pioneer who is now chairman of the board of the SETI Institute; David Grinspoon, a principal scientist in the Department of Space Studies at the Southwest Research Institute and author of *Lonely Planets: The Natural Philosophy of Alien Life;* Christopher McKay, a planetary scientist at NASA's Ames Research Center; and moderator Michael Meyer, senior scientist for astrobiology at NASA headquarters. In the following portion of the debate, the scientists discuss the likelihood of there being life in our stellar neighborhood and the odds for and against its being complex life.

Peter Ward: There is a cultural assumption that there are many alien civilizations. This stems in no small way from the famous estimate by [astronomer] Frank Drake—known as the "Drake Equation"—that was later amended by Drake and [astronomer] Carl Sagan. They arrived at an estimate that there are perhaps a million intelligent civilizations in the Milky Way Galaxy alone.

The Drake and Sagan estimate was based on their best guess about the number of planets in the galaxy, the percentage of those that might harbor life, and the percentage of planets on which life not only could exist but could have advanced to culture. Since our galaxy is but one of hundreds of billions of galaxies in the universe, the number of intelligent alien species would be numbered in the billions. Surely, if there are so many intelligent aliens out there, then the

NASA Panel Discussion, "Great Debates: 'Rare Earth' Parts I, III and IV," *Astrobiology Magazine*, www.astrobio.net, July 15–July 24, 2002.

number of planets with life must be truly astronomical. But what if the Drake and Sagan estimates are way off? If, as could be the reality, our civilization is unique in the galaxy, does that mean that there might be much less life in general as well?

In my view, life in the form of microbes or their equivalents is very common in the universe, perhaps more common than even Drake and Sagan envisioned. However, complex life—animals and higher plants—is likely to be far more rare than commonly assumed. Life on Earth evolved from single celled organisms to multicellular creatures with tissues and organs, climaxing in animals and higher plants. But is Earth's particular history of life—one of increasing complexity to an animal grade of evolution—an inevitable result of evolution, or even a common one? Perhaps life is common, but complex life—anything that is multi-cellular—is not.

Christopher McKay: There is no solid evidence of life elsewhere, but several factors suggest it is common. Organic material is widespread in the interstellar medium and in our own solar system. We have found planetary systems around other sun-like stars. On Earth, microbial life appeared very quickly—probably before 3.8 billion years ago. Also, we know that microbial ecosystems can survive in a variety of environments with liquid water and a suitable chemical energy source or sunlight.

These factors suggest that microbial life—the sort of life the dominated Earth for the first two billion years—is widespread in the stellar neighborhood.

It Is Risky to Generalize from One Example

David Grinspoon: It is always shaky when we generalize from experiments with a sample size of one. So we have to be a bit cautious when we fill the cosmos with creatures based on the time scales of Earth history (it happened so fast here, therefore it must be easy) and the resourcefulness of Earth life (they are everywhere where there is water). This is one history, and one example of life. When our arguments rest on such shaky grounds, balancing a house of cards on a one-card foundation, we are in danger of erecting structures formed more by our desires than the "evidence."

Frank Drake: . . . We look at the Earth, and with regards to [the] origin [of life], as best we know, no special or freak circumstances were required. It took water, organics, a source of energy, and a long time. Deep-sea vents are the current favorite and a reasonable place for the origin. But even if they weren't the culprits, the chemists have found a multitude of other pathways that produce the chemistry of life. The challenge seems to be not to find THE pathway, but the one that was the quickest and most productive. The prime point is that nothing special was required. There will be a pathway that works, on Earth and on similar planets. Then, by Occam's Razor [the principle that the simplest explanation is best], the origin of life on Earth is nothing more than the result of normal processes on the planet. Furthermore, life should appear very frequently on other Earth-like planets. There will be microbial life nearby the solar system.

Donald Brownlee: While there is hope and even expectation of nearby extraterrestrial life, the goal of *Rare Earth* was to point out that the universe is fundamentally hostile to life. Most planets and other places in the universe clearly could not support any type of Earth-like creatures. The universe is vast, so there may be many Earth-like places, but they will be widely spaced, and if they are too widely spaced they will be isolated from each other. What fraction of stars harbor Earth-like planets with Earth-like life? Is it one in a hundred, one in a million, or even less? Even the most optimistic have to admit Earth-like environments must be rare.

In our book *Rare Earth*, we suggest that extraterrestrial life is likely to be near but that complex animal-like life is rare and will probably not be found close to us in space. A major question about life relates to the environments needed for its formation and long term evolution. Unfortunately Earth is our only successful example. Predictions of life elsewhere are problematic; presently there is no detectable life elsewhere in the solar system.

There May Be Life Unlike Earth's

David Grinspoon: I am not convinced that the Earth's carbon-in-water example is the only way for the universe to solve the life riddle. I am not talking about silicon, which is a bad idea, but systems of chemical complexity that we have not thought of, which may not manifest themselves at room temperature in our oxygen atmosphere. The universe is consistently more clever than we are, and we learn about complex phenomena, like life, more through exploration than by theorizing and modeling. I think there are probably forms of life out there which use different chemical bases than we, and which we will know about only when we find them, or when they find us.

An obvious rejoinder to this is, "But no one has invented another system that works as well as carbon-in-water." That is true. But to this I would answer, "We did not invent carbon-in-water!" We discovered it. I don't believe that we are clever enough to have thought of life based on nucleic acids and proteins if we hadn't had this example handed to us. This makes me wonder what else the universe might be using for its refined, evolving complexity elsewhere, in other conditions that seem hostile to life as we know it.

Frank Drake: All evidence of the most primitive steps in the first 700 million years of chemical evolution on Earth is apparently lost. We grope towards understanding of that profound gap in our knowledge by working backwards, hypothesizing that there once was an RNA world based on self-catalyzing RNA. But this system evolved from something else, and led to the esoteric DNA-protein world. As David Grinspoon rightly points out, we are not remotely smart enough to hypothesize ab initio the system of the DNA-protein world, or even the RNA world. It was handed to us on a silver platter. This should be a strong warning that we are over our heads when predicting what might have taken place on other worlds. Give us knowledge of another independent origin of life in space, and the doors to great progress in this field may open.

The Odds of Complex Life

Michael Meyer: I presume that we are in agreement that microbial life, at least, may be common in our stellar neighborhood and even may be present on other planets in our Solar System. That being the premise, the probability of complex life elsewhere is then dependent on the probability of the transition from slime to civilization. It happened here, so why not elsewhere? Do you think that complex life should develop on a sizeable fraction of worlds around other stars?

Christopher McKay: As David Grinspoon pointed out earlier, the Earth is our only example of planetary life. This makes it difficult to unravel what is universal and what is accidental about the nature and history of life. Still, one data point is better than none, and when we look at the question of complex life, our one data point seems to say that complex life arose as a result of the rise of free oxygen. If we take this as being generally true, then we can ask the geophysical question: On what types of planets will free oxygen arise and how long will it take to reach high enough levels? . . .

There may be a range of planet types on which oxygen could arise—and therefore complex life. I would hazard a guess that most—maybe two-thirds—of terrestrial planets with life go on to develop complex life at some stage of their history. An optimist's view. . . .

David Grinspoon: Planetary biospheres are complex entitles whose histories are fraught with contingency, accident, and luck. Therefore, the time it took for complex life to arise on Earth is probably much faster than some and much slower than others. We can't stand a mystery without a chief suspect, so we pin the rise of complex life on the rise of oxygen. This may well have factored in, but as Chris pointed out, there is no reason to believe that oxygen rose on Earth as quickly as it might have elsewhere. The rate of plate tectonics is one variable that will change atmospheric history—there are countless others. For example, if Earth had formed less rich in iron, then oxygen would have risen much more quickly because there would not have been as much iron to devour the oxygen. So in other planetary systems that are less metal-rich, creatures might have evolved to levels far beyond our current state.

Peter Ward: On Earth, evolution has undergone a progressive development of ever more complex and sophisticated forms leading ultimately to human intelligence. Complex life—and even intelligence—could conceivably arise faster than it did on Earth. A planet could go from an abiotic state to a civilization in 100 million years, as compared to the nearly 4 billion years it took on Earth. Evolution on Earth has been affected by chance events, such as the configuration of the continents produced by continental drift. Furthermore, I believe that the way the solar system was produced, with its characteristic number and planetary positions, may have had a great impact on the history of life here.

It has always been assumed that attaining the evolutionary grade we call animals would be the final and decisive step. Once we are at this level of evolution, a long and continuous progression toward intelligence should occur. However, recent research shows that while attaining the stage of animal life is one thing, maintaining that level is quite another. The geologic record has shown that once evolved, complex life is subject to an unending succession of planetary disasters, creating what are known as mass extinction events. These rare but devastating events can reset the evolutionary timetable and destroy complex life while sparing simpler life forms. Such discoveries suggest that the conditions allowing the rise and existence of complex life are far more rigorous than are those for life's formation. On some planets, then, life might arise and animals eventually evolve—only to be soon destroyed by a global catastrophe.

Frank Drake: The Earth's fossil record is quite clear in showing that the complexity of the central nervous system—particularly the capabilities of the brain—has steadily increased in the course of evolution. Even the mass extinctions did not set back this steady increase in brain size. It can be argued that extinction events expedite the development of cognitive abilities, since those creatures with superior brains are better able to save themselves from the sudden change in their environment. Thus smarter creatures are selected, and the growth of intelligence accelerates.

We see this effect in all varieties of animals—it is not a fluke that has occurred in some small sub-set of animal life. This picture suggests strongly that, given enough time, a biota can evolve not just one intelligent species, but many. So complex life should occur abundantly.

There is a claim that "among the millions of species which have developed on Earth, only one became intelligent, so intelligence must be a very, very rare event." This is a textbook example of a wrong logical conclusion. All planets in time may produce one or more intelligent species, but they will not appear simultaneously. One will be first. It will look around and find it is the only intelligent species. Should it be surprised? No! Of course the first one will be alone. Its uniqueness—in principal temporary—says nothing about the ability of the biota to produce one or more intelligent species.

If we assume that Earths are common, and that usually there is enough time to evolve an intelligent species before nature tramples on the biota, then the optimistic view is that new systems of intelligent, technology-using creatures appear about once per year. Based on an extrapolation of our own experience, let's make a guess that a civilization's technology is detectable after 10,000 years. In that case, there are at least 10,000 detectable civilizations out there. This is a heady result, and very encouraging to SETI people. On the other hand, taking into account the number and distribution of stars in space, it implies that the nearest detectable civilizations are about 1,000 light years away, and only one in ten million stars may have a detectable civilization. These last numbers create a daunting challenge to those who construct instruments and projects to search for extraterrestrial intelligence. No actual observing program carried out so far has come anywhere close to meeting the requirement of detecting reasonable signals from a distance of 1,000 light years, or of studying 10 million stars with high sensitivity.

How Often Do Stars Have Habitable Planets?

Donald Brownlee: But how often are animal-habitable planets located in the habitable zones of solar mass stars? Of all the stars that have now been shown to have planets, all either have Jupiter-mass planets interior to 5.5 AU [astronomical units] or they have Jupiters [hot, uninhabitable gas giants] on elliptical orbits. It is unlikely that any of these stars could retain habitable zone planets on long-term stable orbits. On the other hand, many of the stars that do not have currently detectable giant planets could have habitable zone planets. But even when rocky planets are located in the right place, will they have the "right stuff" for the evolution and long term survival of animal-like life? There are many "Rare Earth" factors (such as planet mass, abundance of water and carbon, plate tectonics, etc.) that may play important and even critical roles in allowing the apparently difficult transition from slime to civilization.

As is the case in the solar system, animal-like life is probably uncommon in the cosmos. This might even be the case for microbes: how can scientists agree that microbial life is common in our celestial neighborhood when there is no data? Even the simplest life is extraordinarily complicated and until we find solid evidence for life elsewhere, the frequency of life will unfortunately be guesswork. We can predict that some planetary bodies will provide life-supporting conditions, but no one can predict that life will form.

Frank Drake: Only about 5% of the stars that have been studied sufficiently have hot Jupiters or Jupiters in elliptical orbits. The other 95% of the stars studied do not have hot Jupiters, and just what they have is still an open question. The latest discoveries, which depend on observations over a decade or more, are finding solar system analogs. This suggests that 95% of the stars—for which the answers are not yet in—could be similar to our own system. This is reason for optimism among those who expect solar system analogs to be abundant.

David Grinspoon: I think it is a mistake to look at the many specific peculiarities of Earth's biosphere, and how unlikely such a combination of characteristics seems, and to then conclude that complex life is rare. This argument can only be used to justify the conclusion that planets exactly like Earth, with life exactly like Earthlife, are rare.

My cat "Wookie" survived life as a near-starving alley cat and wound up as a beloved house cat through an unlikely series of biographical accidents, which I won't take up space describing but, trust me, given all of the incredible things that had to happen in just the right way, it is much more likely that there would be no Wookie than Wookie. From this I do not conclude that there are no other cats (The Rare Cat Hypothesis), only that there are no other cats exactly like Wookie.

Life has evolved together with the Earth. Life is opportunistic. The biosphere has taken advantage of the myriad strange idiosyncrasies that our planet has to offer. Not only that, life has created many of Earth's weird qualities. So it is easy to look at our biosphere, and the way it so cleverly exploits Earth's peculiar features, and conclude that this is the best of all possible worlds; that only on such a world could complex life evolve. My bet is that many other worlds, with their own peculiar characteristics and histories, co-evolve their own biospheres. The complex creatures on those worlds, upon first developing intelligence and science, would observe how incredibly well adapted life is to the many unique features of their home world. They might naively assume that these qualities, very different from Earth's, are the only ones that can breed complexity.

The Lifetime of Complex Life

Peter Ward: The period of time that one can expect complex life to exist will vary from world to world. Our "Rare Earth" hypothesis is that on most planets, this will be too short a time to allow complexity to arise at all.

Perhaps the fates of Earth and the other planets in our solar system are not typical at all. But still it is certain that all planets as abodes for life age through time, and as they change they eventually lose the ability to sustain life. Sometimes they do so over immense periods of time, sometimes it might be fast. Some die of old age and some are killed off by cosmic catastrophe. But all end eventually. This salient fact must be considered in any reflection about the frequency of life in the cosmos.

For our own star, the flaring into a red giant will be followed by a stellar retreat into a dwarf stage that will last untold billions of years. As astronomers gaze out into the heavens with their powerful telescopes, they see billions of such stellar tombstones. The galaxy is littered with dead stars, the markers of how many dead planets, and of how many dead civilizations that for a time circled these stars when they were young and vigorous? The presence of these stellar grave-yards are thought-provoking reminders that any estimate about the frequency of life in the universe must take into account the fact that once evolved, life has a finite life span on any world. And, like the va-rieties of ages of individuals, the life span of life-covered planets de-pends in large part on a whole slew of characteristics.

Technology Can Increase Lifetime

David Grinspoon: If complex life sometimes leads to sentient life with powers slightly greater than our own at present, then it need not accept "natural" climate evolution as inevitable. Right now we are in the stage of inadvertently altering our global climate, but it is not in-conceivable that we, or someone else, could advance to the stage of purposefully altering climate for the benefit of the biosphere. If that happens, then reports of the death of the habitable zone are greatly exaggerated.

We should at least ponder the possibility that sentient life, once it arises, will not let its planet become uninhabitable quite so easily. As-sume for a second that humans, or our sentient descendants, do not wipe themselves out any time soon, and solve the problems of aster-oid impacts and other threats to long term survival. How hard would it be, with the technology of even 100 years from now, to say nothing of 10,000 or several million years from now, to put up a sunshade and keep the Earth cool from our warming star? Or move to Mars for a while? Once complex life gets just slightly more advanced than we are now, then it becomes quite possible that sentient creatures can alter the habitability of worlds and planetary systems.

Christopher McKay: Based on our own experience, we know that civilization and technology radically change the rules. Even extrapo-lating 1,000 years into the future (a brief instant on the scale of the age of the planet) we can imagine the transforming effect of intelli-gence on the distribution of life in our own solar system and possibly even our region of the galaxy.

Frank Drake: Once a species has developed high technology, there are many strategies for dealing with the changing brightness of the home star. It has even been suggested by Gregory Benford that the main sequence lifetime of stars can be greatly extended by developing a technology which stirs the star, bringing fresh hydrogen to the core—after all, about 90% of a star's mass is intact when the giant stage is approached. A far out idea to be sure, but it reminds us that clever technologies may be as yet unrecognized by us.

The luminosity of the sun-like stars changes very gradually, over millions of years. This is enough time to mount a massive technologi-cal program to move outwards in the planetary system. Perhaps to ter-raform Mars, or the satellites of Jupiter; perhaps to utilize material from asteroids to build a constellation of space colonies. There is plenty of time, and the motivation will be there. As the sun collapses from the super giant phase, the creatures can move inward, eventually to huddle close to the white dwarf sun. There they will finally be at peace with the cosmos, with a supporting star whose lifetime will be many billions of years.

Is the Universe Bio-Friendly?

Donald Brownlee: There is a common belief that life will always find a way and that the universe itself is bio-friendly. An extension of this line of thinking is that life will usually solve its problems, travel the universe, and perhaps even evolve to something far beyond our "wet life" based on cells, genetic codes, and complex chemical processes. On Earth, life so far has indeed "found the way" and after 4 billion years it has evolved to what we now consider to be normal. But was Earth lucky to get this far? Will its diverse biological communities be able to survive long into the future? Unless the universe actually is bio-friendly, our planet will have barely reached its present state before the ever-warming sun begins to degrade Earth's ability to support plants and vegetarians. Like it or not, this is probably nature's way. Even on the best of planets, advanced life only flourishes for a relatively short period of time.

If advanced life only rarely evolves and doesn't last long when it does, it will be rare in the universe at large. The only way that I see that animals are likely to be common in the universe is if interstellar travel actually is so easy that the Noahs and Johnny Appleseeds of the cosmos just spread things around. I personally doubt that this happens. I believe that it is most likely that organisms as complex as animals only occur in transient cosmic oases widely separated by space and time. Planets form, they may develop life, but eventually the planet and its life perishes. This cycle repeats endlessly in the cosmos. Likewise, civilizations form, they may send SETI transmissions or even launch time capsules, but they will never make direct physical contact.

Intelligent Aliens Are Purely Imaginary

Brian W. Aldiss

Brian W. Aldiss is an eminent science fiction author and critic who lives in England. He wrote the following article for a special issue on astrobiology published by the prestigious British scientific journal *Nature*. In it, Aldiss maintains that the idea of extraterrestrial aliens is no more than a manifestation of the same impulse that has led people throughout history to create myths and fiction about fantastic beings. He believes that the probability of intelligent life emerging on other planets is so low that the search for ETs should not be taken seriously by science.

It is easy to imagine the existence of life elsewhere in the Universe. The key word here is 'imagine'—the human mind has been populated with gods and demons since time immemorial, products of an apparently insatiable craving for the exotic. And still we yearn, our dreams turning from the supernatural and animist to the popular culture of such inventions as Mickey Mouse and Bugs Bunny, Klingons and Vulcans, and, of course, the [movie] *Alien*. The fruitfulness of our imagination is surprising in view of the fact that the Universe itself has offered no help: so far, our search for signs of alien life has drawn a blank. As far as we know, consciousness has dawned nowhere but on our home planet, Earth. I shall argue the case that—for the moment, at least—all other forms of intelligent life are imaginary, as they always have been.

The case that intelligent life is rare in the Universe is logical, yet it is hardly more than a century old, and showing signs of waning in the face of scientific initiatives such as the founding of the NASA Astrobiology Institute, whose aim is to explore the conditions for life on Earth and elsewhere, and even in the commission of this article for a *Nature* Insight entitled 'Astrobiology—Life in the Universe', in which the possibilities of life elsewhere in the Universe are discussed by serious, professional scientists. In the face of millennia of desperation to find aliens, recent scepticism, such as [astronomer Donald] Brownlee and [geologist Peter] Ward's book *Rare Earth*, might be taken for a *fin-de-siècle* aberration.

Brian W. Aldiss, "Desperately Seeking Aliens," *Nature*, vol. 409, February 22, 2001, pp. 1,080–82. Copyright © 2001 by Macmillan Magazines Ltd. Reproduced by permission.

A History of Belief

Serious speculation about life elsewhere was once commonplace. A few centuries ago, many scholars believed that intelligent life existed everywhere, and that an all-powerful God in his generosity had bestowed life on all the planets of the Solar System. This belief had firmest tenure on our neighbouring heavenly body, the Moon. We cannot tell how ancient this erroneous belief may be, but the first story to be set on the Moon is generally agreed to have been written in the second century AD by Lucian of Samosata, whose *True History* is a satire on travel writing.

Lucian's travellers are carried by a waterspout in a Greek ship to the Moon. There they discover that the King of the Moon and the King of the Sun are at War over the issue of the colonization of Jupiter. Fantastic monsters are employed in battles on both sides. Such adventures have always been popular, at least from recent centuries onwards. One authority, Philip B. Gove, lists 215 books describing voyages to the Moon published in the eighteenth century alone. Modes of transport have varied, from angels to migratory geese.

Science has always provided the most potent fuel for the imagination. Space fiction took off after Galileo published *The Starry Messenger* in 1610, conveying vividly the excitement of the moment when a man first looked through a telescope into space. Not only was the Moon no perfect sphere, as had been always thought, but was "just like the surface of the Earth itself, varied everywhere by mountains and valleys". Following his description of the Moon, Galileo went on to reveal his discovery that "there are not only three, but four, erratic sidereal bodies performing their revolutions round Jupiter". This observation of the four main jovian satellites overturned the old Aristotelian thinking, which had set the Earth at the centre of the Universe. Galileo's name became celebrated beyond his native Italy. No longer was it possible for informed people to believe that the Sun went round the Earth. Henceforth, the heliocentric version of our Solar System would prevail, and bring forth many celestial tales—generally satires or utopias. The telescope fathered both astronomy and fantasy. Just one example was *Man in the Moone* (1638) by the learned Bishop Francis Godwin of Hereford, which remained in print for more than two centuries and was much translated. Possibly because the bishop considered his book went against the teachings of the Church, it had to await publication until after his death.

That life in the Universe was, well, universal was taken for granted in the scientific sphere until well into the nineteenth century. William Whewell, the scientist who famously coined the word "scientist', found it necessary to dispute the belief in universal life. His book *Of the Plurality of Worlds* was published anonymously in 1855. Not that Whewell's views did anything to stem the tide of aliens in fiction. Since the days of [science fiction author] H.G. Wells, when cars replaced horses, writers have propagated aliens with increasing assurance. If aliens do not exist, it seems necessary to invent them. It is a nice irony of modern life that the prospects of finding real-life aliens have dimmed just as the 'realism' of fictional aliens has waxed. Perhaps the two are connected—and yet the pendulum could be swinging back sharply.

By the late 1950s, the idea of intelligent life on Mars or any other planet was unfashionable enough to be the subject of derision. The tide turned just two weeks after the Astronomer Royal, Sir Harold Spencer Jones, announced in 1957 that space travel was bunk—when the Soviet Union sent up the first Sputnik. (Jones later compounded his error by saying that he was talking about science fiction.) Once it was generally realized that large objects could travel through space, propelled by rocket motors, the gates were open for speculation about visits and visitations to and from Earth. It was a technological dream. From then onwards, it seemed that most people in the West believed—as had the ancients—that all about us were unseen planets of stars abounding with life. For all Whewell's work, the notion of plurality of interplanetary life had returned. By the early 1960s, unthinking scepticism had turned to unthinking belief.

Earth's Neighbours and Beyond

Nothing except statistics supports the idea that life (or at least intelligent life) exists anywhere else but the Earth. The evidence in our own Solar System is decisively negative. The Moon as an abode of life was ruled out when it was discovered that it had no atmosphere. Elimination next for our shrouded neighbour Venus, of which the Swedish astronomer, Svante Arrhenius, deduced in 1917 that "everything on Venus is dripping wet". The surface, according to Arrhenius, was covered by swamps, in which low forms of life existed: "the organisms are nearly of the same kind all over the planet". (In a forgotten novel of 1956, *Escape to Venus*, S. Makepeace Lott is nearer the mark, speaking of "the battering of the gas storms which flung the suspended dust particles across the face of the planet at several hundred kilometres an hour".) With a mean surface temperature of 740 K, Venus is an unlikely abode of life.

So to Mars, the planet on which most expectations of finding life were pinned. In 1909, astronomer Percival Lowell—self-delusive finder of martian canals—published the well-reasoned *Mars as the Abode of Life*. It must have seemed reasonable at that period to believe in life on our dry neighbouring planet, when the previous century had uncovered evidence of a staggering abundance of life, never previously dreamed of and flourishing over millions of years, in the strata of terrestrial rock. If a monstrous fossil reptile in the ancient sandstone, why not a little green man on Mars?

But no. Since Lowell's day, Mariners and Vikings have called on

Mars. Dust and rocks are all they have found. Mars is a bleak, stony place: dry, with only the thinnest of atmospheres. Viking revealed the martian surface as a highly inhospitable environment for life. The finding of microscopic impressions in a meteorite, believed to be of martian origin, and which might, in some circumstances, have been fossils, has been controversial.

Venus, Earth and Mars lie in the Sun's 'comfort zone'. Beyond Mars stretches a gulf of space, with the gas giants beyond it—surely, there can be no hope for life out there? But the Galileo spacecraft has produced strong evidence that beneath the icy and broken surface of Europa, one of the four galilean Moons of Jupiter, lies an ocean, warmed by the gravitational pull of Jupiter. What might we anticipate there? Intelligent shrimps? Intellectual fish? We can but hope—but there is still a line to be drawn between hope and conviction.

And beyond the Solar System? Our Galaxy contains approximately 200 billion stars. Surely some of them must have planets that sustain life? It is not an unreasonable conjecture, given the numbers. Although we have no evidence that any of the now several dozen known extrasolar planetary systems have suitable conditions for life of the kind we might recognize as such, the numbers could give us hope.

Improbable Evolution of Intelligence

But statistical casuistry works both ways, as is shown by the improbability of intelligent life appearing on the only planet we know well—the Earth. Although life appeared on Earth at least 3.8 billion years ago, not long after the planet itself formed . . . it took another 3.2 billion years before the appearance of complex, multicellular life forms large enough to be viewed without a microscope. Intelligence (as we perhaps mistakenly understand it) has developed only in the past few tens of thousands of years. According to Ward and Brownlee, microbial life in our Galaxy might be common, but complex, multicellular life will be extremely rare.

Each of the steps—between the appearance of life and the evolution of intelligence—reveals its complexity, helped on or deterred by coincidences and catastrophes. Moreover, there might have been only one time propitious for creating the rudiments of life: later might have been too late. Given its evolution through a number of precarious episodes, we perceive that 'intelligent life' is an uncharacteristic effect, not merely in our own Solar System but more universally. In fact, it seems utterly improbable—elsewhere as well as here.

This knowledge has not deterred serious-minded people from attempting to make contact with intelligences elsewhere in the Galaxy. The Search for Extraterrestrial Intelligence (SETI) programme was set up in the 1960s, although so far no one or nothing has answered its signals. . . . Nor have we heard any signals from elsewhere.

A challenge to the consensus of universal biological ubiquity was presented in 1986 by [astrophysicist] John D. Barrow and [physicist] Frank J. Tipler in *The Anthropic Cosmological Principle*, a powerful sequel to Whewell's argument. Using many disciplines, the authors argue that, by an element of design, ours is the only planet that houses cognate beings. Their argument is complex, encompassing the stability of stars and the eccentricities of water, on which life and its origins depend heavily. In sum, it leaves human cognition with a large responsibility for acting as the consciousness of the Universe.

[Anthropologist] C.O. Lovejoy is quoted as saying: "Man is not only a unique animal, but the end product of a completely unique evolutionary pathway, the elements of which are traceable at least to the beginnings of the Cenozoic. This pathway is defined by the evolutionary biologist Ernst Mayr. Speaking of the principal divisions (or phyla) in the animal kingdom, he says that the kingdom "consists of about 25 major branches . . . Only one of them developed real intelligence, the chordates. There are numerous classes in the chordates, I would guess more than 50 of them, but only one of them (the mammals) developed real intelligence, as in Man. The mammals consist of 20-odd orders. Only one of them, the primates, acquiring intelligence, and among the well over 100 species of primates only one, Man, has the kind of intelligence that would permit the development of advanced technology . . . An evolution of intelligence is not probable."

The Blessings of Science

We understand that optimism and imagination help to propel science. Nevertheless, we are entitled to ask whether assumptions about alien life are unscientific. Aliens are the staple diet of modern entertainment, but these are, in the main, contemporary fairy stories, and none the worse for that. However, their relationship with real science is ambiguous. Imaginary aliens are many and diverse, but provide little help in any current comprehension of understanding the Universe: rather than assisting us, aliens impede understanding. Their air of seeming rationality, of being the product of scientific thinking, is spurious. Where, then, do aliens originate, and how has our desperate search for aliens come to find itself on any serious scientific agenda?

An intimacy with the non-human is a fundamental human trait. A vast population of ghosts, ghouls and other mythical creatures his accompanied humankind through the ages, haunting its woods, houses and graveyards. Among their attractions is that they are free of the physical laws that govern humans. In particular, they are at least partly immune to gravity and death (a tradition continued among mythical cartoon creatures such as Tom and Jerry). . . .

We do not believe in fairies any more, nor do we find it necessary to blaspheme against Baal. But it seems that we are born animists. Parents heap a variety of totemistic animals on their children: *Tyrannosaurus rex* is to be found sharing the cot with Winnie the Pooh. As children talk to their stuffed toys, so adults talk to their pets . . .

The latest manifestation of this creaking floorboard in the brain, the alien arriving here from outer space, is the most interesting. Such an event could conceivably happen, and may be regarded indulgently as more supposition than superstition. Much work has been done to render this magical visit plausible. In the 1960s television drama *A for Andromeda*, written by John Elliott and Fred Hoyle, radio signals emanating from the Andromeda Galaxy are picked up by the then new radio telescope at Jodrell Bank, near Manchester, United Kingdom. The signals include directions for the construction of a computer. This computer enables the scientists to build a beautiful alien woman (the first appearance on our screens of Julie Christie). *A for Andromeda*, broadcast hardly an eyeblink beyond the launch of the first Sputnik, marks the emergence of alien life from fantasy into cool scientific reality, given the blessing of a computer. Science fiction infiltrates science itself.

Julie Christie, if memory serves, was gracious and a source of wisdom in her alien avatar. Sometimes, aliens arrive to save us from our own follies. More frequently, they come to invade and destroy us. Such thinking forms a continuity with our ancient dreads of demons, ever hostile to human life.

Let us suppose that aliens are, as I have suggested, merely the latest example of a form of animism at work: or possibly the immature echoes of our own selves, free of time and gravity. So let us suppose further that no one will ever visit or call—because no one is there to call. We, the entire riotous biomass of Earth, are alone on our small planet.

The implications of such a situation are formidable. Scientifically and philosophically, a change of attitude would be demanded. In *A Defence of Poetry* (1821), [Percy Bysshe] Shelley states that "man, having enslaved the elements, remains himself a slave". Could we but free ourselves from those atavistic fancies here enumerated, humankind might consider it not impossible that we should go into the Galaxy with the intention of becoming its consciousness.

LIFE MAY HAVE EXISTED ON MARS

Henry Bortman

Henry Bortman is the managing editor of NASA's online *Astrobiology Magazine*. In the following selection he discusses what kind of microbes might live under the conditions now believed to exist on Mars. Because life on Mars, if it ever emerged, may not have evolved along the same lines as life on Earth, Bortman maintains that Mars landers can't be designed to look for any specific organism, and the current ones aren't equipped to search for life at all. But the discovery that liquid water was once present on the Martian surface means, in Bortman's view, that living organisms might have been there, too.

Was Mars once a living world? Does life continue, even today, in a holding pattern, waiting until the next global warming event comes along? Many people would like to believe so. Scientists are no exception. But so far no evidence has been found that convinces even a sizable minority of the scientific community that the red planet was ever home to life. What the evidence does indicate, though, is that Mars was once a habitable world. Life, as we know it, could have taken hold there.

The discoveries made by NASA's Opportunity rover at Eagle Crater . . . [in 2004] leave no doubt that the area was once "drenched" in water. It might have been shallow water. It might not have stuck around for long. And billions of years might have passed since it dried up. But liquid water was there, at the Martian surface, and that means that living organisms might have been there, too.

So suppose that Eagle Crater—or rather, whatever land formation existed in its location when water was still around—was once alive. What type of organism might have been happy living there?

Probably something like bacteria. Even if life did gain a foothold on Mars, it's unlikely that it ever evolved beyond the Martian equivalent of terrestrial single-celled bacteria. No dinosaurs; no redwoods; no mosquitoes—not even sponges, or tiny worms. But that's not much of a limitation, really. It took life on Earth billions of years to evolve beyond single-celled organisms. And bacteria are a hardy lot.

Henry Bortman, "Life on Mars: A Definite Possibility," *Astrobiology Magazine*, www.astrobio.net, August 30, 2004.

They are amazingly diverse, various species occupying extreme niches of temperature from sub-freezing to above-boiling; floating about in sulfuric acid; getting along fine with or without oxygen. In fact, there are few habitats on Earth where one or another species of bacterium can't survive.

What kind of microbe, then, would have been well adapted to the conditions that existed when Eagle Crater was soggy? Benton Clark III, a Mars Exploration Rover (MER) science team member, says his "general favorite" candidates are the sulfate-reducing bacteria of the genus *Desulfovibrio*. Microbiologists have identified more than 40 distinct species of this bacterium.

Eating Rocks

We tend to think of photosynthesis as the engine of life on Earth. After all, we see green plants nearly everywhere we look and virtually the entire animal kingdom is dependent on photosynthetic organisms as a source of food. Not only plants, but many microbes as well, are capable of carrying out photosynthesis. They're photoautotrophs: they make their own food by capturing energy directly from sunlight.

But *Desulfovibrio* is not a photoautotroph; it's a chemoautotroph. Chemoautotrophs also make their own food, but they don't use photosynthesis to do it. In fact, photosynthesis came relatively late in the game of life on Earth. Early life had to get its energy from chemical interactions between rocks and dirt, water, and gases in the atmosphere. If life ever emerged on Mars, it might never have evolved beyond this primitive stage.

Desulfovibrio makes its home in a variety of habitats. Many species live in soggy soils, such as marshes and swamps. One species was discovered all snug and cozy in the intestines of a termite. All of these habitats have two things in common: there's no oxygen present; and there's plenty of sulfate available.

Sulfate reducers, like all chemoautotrophs, get their energy by inducing chemical reactions that transfer electrons between one molecule and another. In the case of *Desulfovibrio*, hydrogen donates electrons, which are accepted by sulfate compounds. *Desulfovibrio*, says Clark, uses "the energy that it gets by combining the hydrogen with the sulfate to make the organic compounds" it needs to grow and to reproduce.

The bedrock outcrop in Eagle Crater is chock full of sulfate salts. But finding a suitable electron donor for all that sulfate is a bit more troublesome. "My calculations indicate [that the amount of hydrogen available is] probably too low to utilize it under present conditions," says Clark. "But if you had a little bit wetter Mars, then there [would] be more water in the atmosphere, and the hydrogen gas comes from the water" being broken down by sunlight.

So water was present; sulfate and hydrogen could have as an energy source. But to survive, life as we know it needs one more ingredient: carbon. Many living things obtain their carbon by breaking down the decayed remains of other dead organisms. But some, including several species of *Desulfovibrio*, are capable of creating organic material from scratch, as it were, drawing this critical ingredient of life directly from carbon dioxide (CO_2) gas. There's plenty of that available on Mars.

All this gives reason to hope that life that found a way to exist on Mars back in the day when water was present. No one knows how long ago that was. Or whether such a time will come again. It may be that Mars dried up billions of years ago and has remained dry ever since. If that is the case, life is unlikely to have found a way to survive until the present.

Tilting Toward Life

But Mars goes through cycles of obliquity, or changes in its orbital tilt. Currently, Mars is wobbling back and forth between 15 and 35 degrees' obliquity, on a timescale of about 100,000 years. But every million years or so, it leans over as much as 60 degrees. Along with these changes in obliquity come changes in climate and atmosphere. Some scientists speculate that during the extremes of these obliquity cycles, Mars may develop an atmosphere as thick as Earth's, and could warm up considerably. Enough for dormant life to reawaken.

"Because the climate can change on long terms," says Clark, ice in some regions on Mars periodically could "become liquid enough that you would be able to actually come to life and do some things—grow, multiply, and so forth—and then go back to sleep again" when the thaw cycle ended. There are organisms on Earth that, when conditions become unfavorable, can form "spores which are so resistant that they can last for a very long time. Some people think millions of years, but that's a little controversial."

Desulfovibrio is not such an organism. It doesn't form spores. But its bacterial cousin, *Desulfotomaculum*, does. "Usually the spores form because there's something missing, like, for example, if hydrogen's not available, or if there's too much [oxygen], or if there's not sulfate. The bacteria senses that the food source is going away, and it says, 'I've got to hibernate,' and will form the spores. The spores will stay dormant for extremely long periods of time. But they still have enough machinery operative that they can actually sense that nutrients are available. And then they'll reconvert again in just a matter of hours, if necessary, to a living, breathing bacterium, so to speak. "It's pretty amazing," says Clark.

That is not to say that future Mars landers should arrive with life-detection equipment tuned to zero in on species of *Desulfovibrio* or *Desulfotomaculum*. There is no reason to believe that life on Mars, if it ever emerged, evolved along the same lines as life on Earth, let alone that identical species appeared on the two planets. Still, the capabilities of various organisms on Earth indicate that life on Mars—including dormant organisms that could spring to life again in another few hundred thousand years—is certainly possible.

Clark says that he doesn't "know that there's any organism on Earth that could really operate on Mars, but over a long period of time, as the Martian environment kept changing, what you would expect is that whatever life had started out there would keep adapting to the environment as it changed."

Detecting such organisms is another matter. Don't look for it to happen any time soon. Spirit and Opportunity were not designed to search for signs of life, but rather to search for signs of habitability. They could be rolling over fields littered with microscopic organisms in deep sleep and they'd never know it. Even future rovers will have a tough time identifying the Martian equivalent of dormant bacterial spores.

"The spores themselves are so inert," Clark says, "it's a question, if you find a spore, and you're trying to detect life, how do you know it's a spore, [and not] just a little particle of sand? And the answer is: You don't. Unless you can find a way to make the spore do what's called germinating, going back to the normal bacterial form." That, however, is a challenge for another day.

CHAPTER 2

CAN SCIENCE FIND EVIDENCE OF EXTRATERRESTRIAL CIVILIZATIONS?

Contemporary Issues
Companion

SETI Is a Worthwhile Effort

H. Paul Shuch

H. Paul Shuch is the executive director of the SETI League, an international alliance of amateur and professional radio-astronomers and others engaged in grassroots SETI research. In the following selection he summarizes the current status of SETI, the astronomical search for extraterrestrial intelligence, and offers his opinion about its future progress. Shuch suggests that instead of just searching for microwave beacons, astronomers should be looking for other types of signaling technologies, perhaps even evidence of interstellar probes or feats of alien astroengineering. He also explains why he believes Earth has nothing to lose by listening for signals from advanced ET civilizations.

We were the only game in town—the sole sentient species in the cosmos. Or, so the mainstream scientific community thought in 1959. That perception wouldn't hold for long, however. Less than half a century later, scientific evidence would suggest that our civilization could be but one among many.

In 1959, young radio astronomer Frank Drake was fresh out of graduate school when he hit upon a seemingly ludicrous idea. Why not use his employer's radio telescope to search for intelligently generated signals from the stars? He cautioned himself to do so quietly; this science-fiction search might well be professional suicide. So he set to work, quietly assembling a crude, one-channel listening station to train on two nearby, sunlike stars.

Then, the 1959 Cocconi and Morrison article came out. In a brief paper in the scientific journal *Nature*, two Cornell professors, Giuseppe Cocconi and Philip Morrison, proposed the very search that Drake was setting out to perform. This is a prime example of what I call the Parenthood Principle: When a great idea is ready to be born, it goes out in search of a parent. Sometimes, it finds more than one. Now Schrödinger's cat was out of the bag, and Drake had to go public. But discretion still ruled the day. Even the first detection, of a classified military aircraft, was of necessity held close to the chest.

Today, the search for extraterrestrial intelligence (SETI) has emerged

H. Paul Shuch, "The Search for Extraterrestrial Intelligence," *Futurist*, vol. 37, May/ June 2003, pp. 52–55. Copyright © 2003 by the *Futurist*. Reproduced by permission.

out of the fringes into the scientific mainstream. In 40 years, researchers have developed technologies the likes of which young Drake could scarcely have dreamed. As Drake grayed into the elder statesman of an established scientific discipline, thousands of people have conducted hundreds of searches for our cosmic companions, scanning billions of microwave and optical channels and spending millions of dollars in the process. SETI is no longer a four-letter word. But for all of that effort, we are today no more successful in detecting extraterrestrial intelligence than Drake was with his first search.

We can improve our chances for success by redefining SETI. At present, SETI is as narrowly focused as the spectral emissions that we hope to intercept. What began as a search for microwave beacons should be expanded to encompass all signaling technologies, whether or not we have achieved them yet at our present level of societal and technical adolescence.

Might we someday launch robotic interstellar probes? If so, then we should have an organized strategy for seeking out such probes launched by more-advanced societies. Can we imagine the day when we will be capable of great feats of astroengineering? Then our present efforts should include a search for the engineering marvels of our more-capable neighbors. Might our own starships someday leave a detectable residue? Then the search for the advanced propulsion signatures of others should be on our agenda. If we can imagine it, then we should be looking for it. . . .

Nothing to Lose by Listening

A common myth holds that our brothers and sisters in space will hand us a silver platter loaded with solutions to all of humankind's problems: cures for disease and poverty and ignorance and prejudice, which *everyone* knows are trivial matters for those advanced beings conquering the interstellar gulf.

Everyone is most likely wrong. Since ours is a relatively young planet orbiting a fairly new star, it's a cinch to speculate that we're the newcomers on the block. Top astrophysicists have estimated that other civilizations could well be anywhere from a thousand to a billion years older than our own. If the first extraterrestrial civilization we encounter is at the upper end of that age continuum, SETI scientists will be lucky to even recognize its artifacts as manifestations of intelligence, let alone interpret them. Such an ancient race would be as far ahead of us as we are beyond bacteria.

We will be far better served if our cosmic communicators have advanced only a little bit beyond us. If they lead us by, let us say, a million years, then they might make their culture known to us much as we communicate with household pets. This is speculative to be sure, but what if they regard us much as we regard dogs? What do we stand to gain? And to lose?

One could argue that *Canis familiaris* (domestic dog) enjoys a longer life span and better nutrition than his wild ancestor; that by taking him under our protection, humans have given him a higher standard of living. Pulling our sleds, herding our sheep, guarding our children, and leading our blind are small prices for him to pay for the benefits we benevolently bestow. But did anyone ever bother to ask Fido how he feels about the arrangement?

Science fiction is full of cautionary tales of humanity being subdued and subjugated by advanced aliens. Surely if their technology is capable of announcing its presence across the cosmic gulf, they have the capacity to come here in conquest. Better to let well enough alone, some argue.

But wait—SETI is all about communication, *not* contact. Unless we've got the laws of nature all wrong, beings of an advanced civilization at the far end of the galaxy will still take 50,000 to 70,000 years to get here, assuming they want to know about us. That distant cousin of yours in Kansas receiving your Christmas card might just take your casual "drop by sometime" seriously and show up on your doorstep next Thanksgiving, but extraterrestrial beings? Not likely.

For one thing, they haven't been invited. We inhabit a paranoid planet. Pressures from governing bodies and private citizens alike have prompted most scientific organizations and SETI research facilities to adopt a policy that prohibits interstellar transmission lest we give ourselves away. With only a few minor exceptions, we have refrained from shouting in the jungle. The act of listening in no way reveals our position or our interest; it makes us no more vulnerable to invasion and domination than we would by turning a deaf ear to the universe. Given that SETI is a passive activity, it would seem we have nothing to lose in listening.

And everything to gain.

One Is the Loneliest Number

I've skipped over that other alternative: that we could well encounter a civilization just a little bit more advanced than ours—one that, in its recent history, has beaten its exo-swords into exo-plowshares. One that has learned, in generations not too remote, to harness its planet's resources in an environmentally responsible way, to embrace genetic engineering with compassion and reason, to ensure the survival of its species through cooperation rather than conflict. These are lessons we need to learn if we are to survive the next thousand years or so and thus to reach their level. If we're incredibly fortunate, their transmissions might contain their own social and cultural history, including a glimpse into their crossroads and crises. But even lacking such details, a signal received from such a society will testify to life's capacity for survival against long odds. We would do well to learn from their example.

Part of that example is in the medium itself. If beings from a modestly advanced civilization choose to fling photons our way, then we can conclude that they have deemed it safe to do so. Here, too, we might do well to learn from their example by abandoning our planetary paranoia and beginning to transmit warm greetings to other young civilizations near our point on the developmental continuum. Should the phone happen to ring, etiquette demands we answer it pleasantly.

What of the inherent dangers in making our presence known? Here we can be a bit philosophical. There is danger if they know about us. There is danger if they don't know about us. The universe is a dangerous place. Of course, that's no reason to hide under a rock (or to remain on our own rock). It is human (and, I presume, alien) nature to confront danger head on in the pursuit of knowledge.

It could well be that we are at the midpoint of that pursuit. If technology continues to advance as it has in the past, 40 years from now will likely see another billionfold increase in search space. Perhaps that's what it's going to take to achieve SETI success. This field of study offers little to anyone who demands instant gratification. Lest we become discouraged, we should remember that the 40 years since Drake's first search constitute a mere eyeblink in human history.

What Will Four More Decades Bring?

Where will SETI be in four more decades? Thus far, human technological progress (which SETI both reflects and stimulates) has been exponential. Like the expanding universe hypothesis, we have insufficient data to detect any slowing of that trend. In all likelihood, our receivers will soon span the electromagnetic spectrum, from radio through microwaves into the infrared, across the visible, ultraviolet, X-ray, gamma ray, and cosmic ray spectra, all in real time. We are developing technologies today that will enable us to see in all directions at once. Forty years from now we will be scanning farther out in time and space than Drake ever deemed possible. If there are electromagnetically polluting civilizations out there, surely we will have detected their photonic debris by then.

Or perhaps not. It could well be that as civilizations advance they become, by design or chance, effectively invisible. In that case, 40 years from now we'll have arrived at an epiphany: We are not alone, but we might as well be.

How might such an understanding impact on our view of humanity's place in the cosmos? My guess is that it would send us back to 40 years ago, when we were the only game in town.

SETI WILL FAIL

Ben Zuckerman

Ben Zuckerman is a professor of physics and astronomy at the University of California, Los Angeles. He has co-edited six books, including (with Michael Hart) *Extraterrestrials: Where Are They?* In the following article he argues that because astronomers are now on the verge of being able to detect Earthlike planets, more advanced civilizations would surely have had that capability long ago and would have come to investigate Earth. Zuckerman believes that SETI enthusiasts have failed to take this into account. In his opinion, the absence of evidence that extraterrestrials have visited means that there are no advanced civilizations in this region of the galaxy and that the search for such signals is therefore a waste of time.

Where do humans stand on the scale of cosmic intelligence? For most people, this question ranks at or very near the top of the list of "scientific things I would like to know." Lacking hard evidence to constrain the imagination, optimists conclude that technological civilizations far in advance of our own are common in our Milky Way Galaxy, whereas pessimists argue that we Earthlings probably have the most advanced technology around. Consequently, this topic has been debated endlessly and in numerous venues.

Unfortunately, significant new information or ideas that can point us in the right direction come along infrequently. But recently I have realized that important connections exist between space astronomy and space travel that have never been discussed in the scientific or popular literature. These connections dearly favor the more pessimistic scenario mentioned above.

Serious radio searches for extraterrestrial intelligence (SETI) have been conducted during the past few decades. Brilliant scientists have been associated with SETI, starting with pioneers like Frank Drake and the late Carl Sagan and then continuing with Paul Horowitz, Jill Tarter, and the late Barney Oliver. Even with all their accumulated talent, these investigators have failed to consider the full implications for SETI of all advanced civilizations possessing space telescopes capa-

Ben Zuckerman, "Why SETI Will Fail," *Mercury*, vol. 31, September/October 2002, pp. 14–22. First appeared in *Mercury Magazine* and is used with permission of *Mercury* and the Astronomical Society of the Pacific. Reproduced by permission.

ble of discovering nearby living worlds. A very likely consequence of such discoveries will be interstellar travel to investigate the nature of alien life forms. The fact that, evidently, no technological creatures have come to investigate Earth during the past several billions of years is strong evidence that few such creatures exist in our galaxy.

Identifying Living Worlds

Detection of extrasolar Jupiter-like planets . . . is all the rage these days. But to find out more about where we rank on the cosmic intelligence scale, we need to learn about the preponderance and properties of extrasolar Earth-like planets. To do this, we need to launch moderate-sized telescopes into space. . . .

According to the timetable envisioned for NASA's Terrestrial Planet Finder (TPF) mission, in the next 20 years we should witness the deployment of space telescopes capable of spotting Earth-like planets orbiting nearby stars. As currently conceived, these telescopes will be able to measure mid-infrared spectra of planetary atmospheres and detect molecules such as water vapor, carbon dioxide, methane, and free oxygen in the form of ozone. In other words, TPF will be capable of identifying life-bearing planets within about 30 light-years of Earth. When technology improves during the coming centuries, the range of such telescopes will no doubt be extended out to 100 or more light-years.

Less than 50 years will separate the beginning of serious SETI efforts and the construction of space telescopes able to detect and study nearby Earths. We therefore live in a unique moment of human history in which we possess powerful ground-based radio telescopes but no TPF. We are an infant technological civilization in this 50 year period, which is an infinitesimal time interval measured in any cosmic context. If we can build TPF so soon after becoming technological and beginning SETI, then other technological civilizations should have little trouble building their own versions of TPF. And SETI pessimists and optimists alike agree that if technological civilizations are numerous in the Milky Way, then a typical civilization must live for a very long time, on the order of millions of years.

Therefore, SETI endeavors should assume that any technological civilization within a few hundred light-years has had space telescopes capable of detecting and studying Earth for quite some time. If the typical technological civilization is 1 million years old, then such a civilization, if it lies within a few hundred light-years, has been studying us with its space telescopes for the past million years. This article will consider some implications of this basic idea.

At present, various radio and optical SETI programs, including the sensitive, ambitious, and relatively expensive Project Phoenix of the SETI institute, are targeting nearby Sun-like stars. Project Phoenix, led by Jill Tarter, is searching 1,000 nearby stars using telescopes at a pair of widely separated radio observatories to help discriminate against human-made interference. The Phoenix search primarily uses the 305-meter Arecibo telescope in Puerto Rico and the 76-meter Jodrell Bank telescope in Britain.

Rather than hunt blindly for signals coming from nearby stars, the Phoenix team could use its telescope time more economically if it skipped over such stars. Instead, Project Phoenix should target more distant stars that will remain out of range of TPF and its immediate successors—for example stars in the plane of the Milky Way or in the Andromeda Galaxy. Then, a few decades from now, radio and optical SETI programs could intensively focus upon promising planetary systems identified by TPF.

Is E.T. Passive?

Even if TPF discovers a favorably arranged planetary system or, better yet, a living planet whose atmospheric composition resembles that of Earth, the chance that the planet hosts a technological civilization is minuscule. I'll explain why.

Our nearest stellar neighbors have been and will remain our nearest neighbors for a million years or longer. Because the Sun is traveling at about 10 kilometers per second with respect to most nearby stars, it will take millions of years for Earth to move 100 light-years with respect to these stars.

Suppose that a million years ago Earth entered the sphere of detectability of the space telescopes of an advanced civilization on a planet now within 100 light-years of Earth. Using their own version of TPF, the inhabitants would have discovered Earth and the fact that it is a life-bearing planet. They would then have pointed some large telescopes at Earth and tried SETI. But the search would have been fruitless because we technological humans were still a million years in the future.

After decades or centuries of unsuccessful SETI, these extraterrestrials would have a decision to make. They might have decided to sit passively as our planetary system drifted by theirs. Such passivity is implicit in a SETI search scheme outlined by Andrew Howard and Paul Horowitz in which, ironically, TPF would be used to detect "deliberate laser transmissions from a technologically advanced civilization" within about 50 light-years of Earth. But these authors fail to consider that the advanced civilization surely would have discovered our living Earth long, long ago, and Howard and Horowitz certainly failed to consider the likely consequences of such a discovery.

Advanced extraterrestrials would have a more attractive and much more plausible alternative to long-term passivity: They could send an interstellar spaceship that contained themselves, or robots, or both, to explore our living Earth. Everything we know about human nature and history indicates that intelligent creatures will follow this path. Exploration of our solar system began with telescopic observations from Earth. But as soon as we developed the capability, we launched spaceships to explore planets and moons up close because observing from afar is limited and, ultimately, unsatisfying. Without going there, how will we ever find out whether there is or ever was life on Mars, Europa, or Titan?

Some SETI proponents, notably Frank Drake and Barney Oliver, have disparaged interstellar spaceships as being slow and expensive compared with radio waves. But intelligent beings aren't going to sit around their home planet for millions of years beaming radio waves into the galaxy. They are going to venture out and explore the universe around them. After all, redwood trees, dinosaurs, and whales do not transmit radio waves. So, if we, or technological extraterrestrials, want to discover and study alien life forms, we must physically travel between the stars in spaceships. How else can we ever know if all life is constructed from proteins and nucleic acids, or is carbon based, or uses liquid water for a solvent? If we do not undertake such voyages, then we will forever forfeit the possibility of answering such profound questions for all living worlds that lack a technological civilization, as Earth did for billions of years.

Interstellar Travel

Scientists and nonscientists alike are curious about life in the universe. For example, biologist Penelope Boston, a member of the Mars Society's Board of Directors, stated a few years ago on the Discovery Channel's program *Destination Mars:* "I am a biologist; I have a burning need to know about life in the universe." In 1998, I participated in a NASA-sponsored meeting at Caltech on "Robotic Interstellar Exploration in the 21st Century." The engineers and physical scientists in attendance agreed that if humans decide to fund an interstellar mission, which will cost more than all previous space missions, the motivation will be the prospect of investigating a living world at the end of the voyage. . . .

For interstellar travel to become practical, voyages should take a few hundred years or less, with perhaps 1,000 years as an upper limit. Scientists and engineers have proposed a variety of propulsion schemes (such as nuclear bombs, pellet streams, and lasers) that could accelerate a spaceship to a few percent of the speed of light. If living worlds are so uncommon in the solar vicinity that the nearest one is farther away than 100 light-years, then exploratory voyages over such long distances will take such a long time that civilizations will probably send robots and frozen embryos in preference to creatures of flesh and blood (or whatever they're made of). Should living worlds be rare, widely separated, and thus difficult to reach with spaceships, then communicative technological civilizations will be rarer still and SETI searches of nearby stars will fail.

But even if living worlds are not rare, SETI searches of stars within a few hundred light-years are doomed to fail because an advanced civilization on any nearby planet would have long ago employed space telescopes to identify Earth as a living planet and would have come to our solar system to investigate Earth. And once here, why leave? Just as the Polynesians who discovered Hawai'i after a long and dangerous voyage across the Pacific did not turn around and return to their point of origin, so representatives of a spacefaring civilization will remain in the planetary systems they choose to explore. After all, it's a long way home.

Thus, the only SETI strategy that makes any sense is to search for signals from distant civilizations, where "distant" is defined as far enough away that Earth has never been discovered as an interesting place by the space telescopes of a putative civilization. Signals received from such distant beings are unlikely to have been generated for our benefit, so detection of extraterrestrial intelligence will likely require luck, and round-trip electromagnetic communications will be slow.

Nearby Intelligent Aliens Don't Exist

In summary, three simple and plausible postulates have major implications for SETI. First, soon after the development of technology, all civilizations will build space telescopes capable of measuring the atmospheric compositions of Earth-like worlds at distances of hundreds of light-years. Second, intelligent life is curious about other life forms, whether or not that other life is technological. And third, once having used space telescopes to discover a nearby living planet, most if not all technological civilizations will be sufficiently curious to construct interstellar spaceships to visit that planet. If these postulates are true, the absence of intelligent aliens in our solar system is strong evidence that they do not exist anywhere in our region of the Milky Way and SETI searches of nearby stars are destined to fail.

Regarding the frequency of technological civilizations in our galaxy, the marriage of TPF and interstellar travel may be extended to distant times and places. Oxygen built up in Earth's atmosphere about 2 billion years ago. Following that period, Earth could have been identified as a living world from afar. Any technological civilization that came within a few hundred light-years of Earth during the past 2 billion years would have had to choose between passively floating by (for a million years) and never learning about terrestrial life, or actively sending a spaceship to our solar system.

Even if such an expedition took 1,000 years, this still would have been a very quick trip in comparison to a billion-year wait for humans to show up with radio transmitters. During the past 2 billion years, millions of Sun-like stars have passed within a few hundred light-years of Earth, yet there is no evidence that technological extraterrestrials have ever visited our solar system. This suggests that very few, if any, technological civilizations existed around these millions of stars. Perhaps the origin of life on Earth was a once-in-a-galaxy fluke, or perhaps life almost never evolves to high intelligence, or perhaps civilizations destroy themselves soon after they develop technology. Although technological life must be exceedingly rare, we currently don't understand astronomy or especially biology well enough to know why.

The above picture, which can be extrapolated to the Galaxy as a whole, is completely different from the one painted by [astronomers] William Newman and Carl Sagan in their ambitious 1981 paper "Galactic Civilizations: Population Dynamics and Interstellar Diffusion." There they model the physical dispersal of technological civilizations as a very slow diffusion process for the following reason. Consider a spacefaring technological civilization arising some 200 light-years from Earth. Then, according to Newman and Sagan, "such a civilization will have been intensively occupied in the colonization of more than 200,000 planetary systems before reaching Earth, some 200 light-years away."

Sagan presented a similar argument in his 1980 book *Cosmos*, where he remarked on page 308, "that an advanced interstellar spacefaring civilization would have no reason to think there was something special about the Earth unless it had been here already . . . From their point of view, all nearby star systems are more or less equally attractive for exploration or colonization." These statements ignore the power of TPF. Just as ground-based telescopes pointed the way to intensive spacecraft exploration of the most interesting planets and moons in our solar system, so would a TPF show a technological civilization just which of 200,000 nearby star systems are worthy of direct exploration.

Pessimists Are Optimists and Vice Versa

In conclusion, the relevance of TPF to the question posed at the beginning forcefully drives home the limited predictive powers of scientists and engineers when forecasting our technological future. Like everyone else, Newman and Sagan failed to anticipate the possibility of TPF and its importance in the SETI debate, even though they wrote their paper just a mere decade before TPF became big news in the space astronomy community! This illustrates how foolishly presumptuous it is when SETI proponents exclaim that interstellar travel is impossible or so difficult that it will never happen. "Never" is a very long time. Already, four spaceships (Pioneers 10 and 11, Voyagers 1 and 2) are exiting the solar system less than a century after the airplane was invented.

The ultimate Luddites are those who deny that human destiny is to venture into space, to become the Little Green Men and Women. Rather than being optimists, SETI proponents who deny this future to human beings are the ultimate technological pessimists. While SETI skeptics may envision humans as possessing the most advanced brains in the Milky Way, nonetheless, it is we pessimists who are the true technological optimists.

SCIENTISTS WONDER WHY NO ALIENS HAVE VISITED EARTH

Nikos Prantzos

Nikos Prantzos is a researcher at the Paris Institute of Astrophysics who has written many articles and several books. The following selection is from the English edition of his book *Our Cosmic Future*. In it, Prantzos offers a clear explanation of the famous Fermi Paradox: the conflict between the assumption that advanced extraterrestrials probably exist with the fact that they have not visited Earth. Discussions of extraterrestrial life often refer to the Fermi Paradox and entire books have been written about it, but few analyze its premises as concisely as Prantzos does. As he points out, many different solutions to the paradox have been proposed, yet the debate about them will not end until evidence of an ET civilization is found.

The question of the plurality of worlds has a long and fluctuating history, rich in new developments of a sometimes passionate nature. Some arguments used in the past by supporters and opponents of the ETI hypothesis (ExtraTerrestrial Intelligence) are cause for amusement today. It is quite probable that some of our modern arguments will have the same effect on our descendants in a few decades or centuries to come.

Scientific study of ETI has a short history, going back only forty years. In an article published in 1959 in *Nature*, physicists Giuseppe Cocconi and Phil Morrison suggested that microwaves (high-frequency radio waves) are the best vector for interstellar communication. Not only do these waves penetrate the terrestrial atmosphere, but they can also pass through galactic dust and gas clouds. Visible photons, our traditional window upon the Universe, are absorbed by these clouds. Hence optical telescopes cannot see nearly as far as a radiotelescope across the disk of the Milky Way. In addition, radiotelescopes can survey the skies 24 hours a day, even in broad daylight or under thick cloud cover. As far as X-rays and gamma rays, which are at the high-frequency end of the electromagnetic spectrum, are concerned, our at-

Nikos Prantzos, "Route to the Stars," *Our Cosmic Future: Humanity's Fate in the Universe*, ed. and trans. Stephen Lyle. New York: Cambridge University Press, 2000. Copyright © 2000 by Cambridge University Press. Reproduced by permission of the publisher and author.

mosphere absorbs them and they cannot reach Earth's surface. (This is fortunate, since they are particularly harmful to living organisms.) Microwaves have another advantage: they carry little energy. This means that less energy would be expended in sending a message at these wavelengths. Cocconi and Morrison emphasised a third important point. Our Galaxy radiates little in the microwave region of the spectrum, compared with other radio frequencies. In other words, background noise would not interfere with communications.

The Beginning of SETI

These considerations opened up the modern era in the plurality of worlds debate, by initiating a scientific study of the problem, and the acronym ETI was born. The first to apply these ideas was Frank Drake, the young director of the Green Bank National Radioastronomy Observatory in the USA. He set up the first systematic search for extraterrestrial signals, called Ozma. The project was named after the queen of the imaginary country of Oz, a distant and inaccessible place, peopled with exotic creatures, in the story by Frank Baum. In 1960, the Green Bank radiotelescope spent two months looking for radio signals in the direction of two nearby stars, Epsilon Eridani and Tau Ceti, both about 12 light-years away. The negative results of this first experience did nothing to discourage ETI supporters. Dozens of other projects sprang into being, not only in the USA and the USSR, but also in Canada, Australia, France and Holland. A few thousand hours spent listening to the heavens have revealed nothing to date. The searchers' initial optimism (reflected in the name of these projects: CETI, meaning Communication with ExtraTerrestrial Intelligence) gradually gave way to a more cautious attitude, at which point the project was renamed SETI, or Search for ExtraTerrestrial Intelligence.

Two results have come out of SETI up to the present time. One of them is probably durable and the other is probably temporary. Probes sent out to the distant confines of the Solar System have not indicated any life form in our immediate neighbourhood. Moreover, radiofrequency observation of the sky has not led to any detection of extraterrestrial signals. Given the size of the task, this result should come as no surprise. A much greater effort will be needed before any statistically significant conclusion can be drawn. However, even if we manage, over the next two centuries, to examine each of the hundred billion stars in our Galaxy across ten billion radio channels, what could we conclude from an absence of any artificial signal? We could only say that none of the supposed civilisations happened to be emitting in our direction. This hardly settles the question about whether ETI exists.

Where Are They?

Apart from these search programmes, there is another observational fact whose importance is difficult to weigh up: the absence of any trace of extraterrestrial civilisation on our planet or elsewhere in the Solar System. This question, already raised by [Bernard de] Fontenelle in his *Conversations on the Plurality of Worlds* [1686], reappeared in its modern version around the middle of the twentieth century.

Towards the end of the 1940s, there came the first wave of reports concerning flying saucers and other UFOs (Unidentified Flying Objects), particularly in the USA. During a visit to the Los Alamos military laboratory in 1950, Italian physicist Enrico Fermi got into discussions on the subject with his colleagues. Among them was Edward Teller, future father of the American H-bomb. Everyone quickly agreed that the UFOs were unlikely to have extraterrestrial origins. The discussion moved on to the more general subject of extraterrestrial civilisations and interstellar travel. It was at this point that Fermi suddenly exclaimed: 'But where are they?' He went on to do a series of calculations to assess the probable number of civilisations in our Galaxy, concluding that they should already have visited us several times by now. In Fermi's view, the complete lack of evidence for such a visit did not necessarily imply that there were no extraterrestrials. It might just mean that insterstellar travel was impossible, or that technological civilisations were too short-lived, plagued by self-destruction upon discovering the secrets of the atom. (It should be remembered that the balance of terror between the USA and the USSR had just begun to hold sway at the time.)

This discussion between Fermi and Teller remained practically unknown for a long time. The question 'Where are they?', generally attributed to Fermi without further comment, first appeared in [astronomer Carl] Sagan and [I.S. Shklovskii's] book *Intelligent Life in the Universe*, in 1966. In 1975, American astronomer Michael Hart independently rediscovered Fermi's arguments, without knowing about the discussion with Teller. His article came to the radical conclusion that the absence of extraterrestrials on Earth implies that we are the only technological civilisation in the Galaxy. He deduced that the continued search for radio signals would be a waste of time and money. Following this provocative article, Carl Sagan referred to this problem as the 'Fermi paradox'.

Hart's pessimistic conclusions began a period of passionate debate on the subject of ETI, notably in the USA. The controversy reached its climax in the early 1980s. In a series of articles, mathematician Frank Tipler observed that Fermi's paradox became even more paradoxical if it were assumed that one of the supposed civilisations were in a position to build self-replicating machines. . . . [Such] machines could completely colonise the whole Galaxy in a relatively short time, quite independently of what was happening to the civilisation which had instigated their dissemination. The fact that there are no such robots in our Solar System is even more significant than the absence of any trace of extraterrestrial signals. In Tipler's view, it proves our technological superiority, if not our total solitude in the Galaxy.

The Assumptions of the Paradox

Any paradox is based on at least one invalid assumption. The logical statement of Fermi's paradox is as follows:

A   Our civilisation is not the only technological civilisation in the Galaxy.

B   Our civilisation is in every way average, or typical. In particular, it is not the first to have appeared in the Galaxy, it is not the most technologically advanced, and it is not the only one seeking to explore the cosmos and communicate with other civilisations.

C   Interstellar travel is not too difficult for civilisations slightly more advanced than our own. Some have mastered this kind of travel and undertaken a galactic colonisation programme, with or without self-replicating robots.

D   Galactic colonisation is a relatively fast undertaking and could be achieved in less than a billion years. This represents only a small fraction of the age of the Milky Way.

If hypotheses A to D are valid, we can clearly deduce that 'They should be here'. The Fermi paradox applies. Supporters of ETI reject at least one of assumptions C and D, and some even go so far as to deny B, in order to save the key hypothesis A. In contrast, their opponents uphold the plausibility of C and D, whilst completely rejecting B. The most extreme even reject hypothesis A.

Why ETs Might Not Come to Earth

This is not the place to go into all the arguments for and against ETI made in the context of Fermi's paradox. Those arguments most often discussed do not refer to the physical aspect of the problem (the feasibility of interstellar travel and construction of self-replicating robots), but rather to its sociological features. Some argue that extraterrestrials would not even be interested in space travel, let alone expansion across the Galaxy. Their civilisation might have quickly turned to a spiritual way of life, occupying itself with contemplation and meditation; or it might have adopted the zero growth rate so dear to ecologists, making space colonisation unnecessary. Others, like Fermi himself, believe that a technological civilisation might be too short-lived, destroying itself before it could solve the problems of interstellar travel.

Such sociological arguments aim to reject hypotheses B and C. There is another class of sociological arguments, generally referred to as the cosmic zoo (or quarantine) hypothesis. According to this view, put forward by American astronomer John Ball in 1973, extraterrestrials have already visited our Solar System, either in the recent or distant past, but prefer to observe us from afar for various reasons. For example, they may consider us too primitive, they may not wish to interfere with our development, or again, they may fear our atomic weapons!

It should be noted that the first person to discuss these issues in the twentieth century seems to have been the Russian savant and father of astonautics Konstantin Tsiolkovsky. He put forward several possible explanations for the lack of evidence to support the claim that there is intelligent extraterrestrial life. For instance, he observed that Europeans discovered native Americans only many thousands of years after the beginning of their civilisation (Fontenelle's argument). But he preferred the so-called zoo hypothesis, which argues that 'we have been set aside as a reserve of intelligence in order to allow our species to evolve to perfection and thereby bring something unique to the cosmic community'.

Would Every Civilisation Act the Same?

All these sociological arguments share a common weak point. It is hard to believe that any one of them could apply to every single extraterrestrial civilisation in the Galaxy. At least one hypothetical civilisation ought to escape self-destruction, solve the problem of space travel and undertake a programme of galactic colonisation. The behaviour of animal species on Earth shows that they always go through an expansion phase, favoured by natural selection, just because this maximises their chances of survival. What is more, at least one of these civilisations ought to have overcome the taboo exhorting them to avoid all contact with our own civilisation. If none has come to this point, then assumption B is implicitly violated. For in this case, we would be the only ones seeking contact with other civilisations.

It is interesting to note that sociological arguments are generally invoked by those who advocate a search for radio signals. There is an obvious inconsistency in this position. Consider one of the first extraterrestrial civilisations wishing to communicate with other forms of intelligence. It would be easy to show that, even in the most favourable case, the closest civilisation would be hundreds or thousands of light-years away. Consequently, no reply would come to their radio signals before several centuries had elapsed. In such conditions, it would seem more logical to invest in a space travel programme. If they explored neighbouring stellar systems using interstellar spacecraft, they would at least possess concrete information after a few centuries, even if there were no other civilisations in existence. A strategy based purely on radio emissions could go without results for thousands of years.

Explaining away Fermi's paradox by sociological arguments seems to me extremely questionable. It would be quite a different matter if there existed a sociological theory explaining why all civilisations must behave in this way. However, I doubt whether such a theory will ever be formulated. I also find it difficult to accept the physical argument invoked by Enrico Fermi in 1950 (during his discussion with Teller), and independently by British astrophysicist Fred Hoyle. In their view, interstellar travel is quite simply impossible. The speculations presented in this [article] are then merely a naive vision of reality, seriously underestimating the difficulties involved. Our species is therefore condemned to remain forever within the confines of the Solar System, until the death of our star. However, no physical law seems to forbid the accomplishment of such journeys. Difficulties are quantitative, rather than qualitative, and it seems unlikely that they will permanently block the way to deep space travel.

Earth Might Have the First Civilisation

The most economical solution to Fermi's paradox consists in straightforwardly rejecting hypothesis A, as proposed by Hart and Tipler: our civilisation might just be the first technological civilisation to have appeared in the Galaxy. This solution is consistent with our present understanding of the theory of evolution, according to which the emergence of intelligence has been a rather improbable event. It is a significant fact that supporters of ETI are mainly astronomers, whilst biologists remain neutral, or openly hostile.

In Tipler's view, the main motivation for proponents of ETI is metaphysical: their hope is that extraterrestrial intervention will save us from ourselves. In his book *Broca's Brain*, Carl Sagan writes: 'It is possible that among the first contents of such a [radio] message may be detailed prescriptions for the avoidance of technological disaster, for a passage through adolescence to maturity.' In the introduction to his anthology *Interstellar Communication*, Canadian astrophysicist Alastair Cameron writes: 'Perhaps we shall also receive valuable lessons in the techniques of stable world government.' The leading light in the search for ETI radio signals, Frank Drake, expresses an almost religious desire in his eloquently titled article *On Hands and Knees in Search of Elysium:*

> It is extremely likely that any civilization we detect would be more advanced than ours. Thus it would provide us with a glimpse of what our own future could be. . . . It is the immortals we will most likely discover. . . . An immortal civilization's best assurance of safety would be to make other societies immortal like themselves, rather than risk hazardous military adventures. Thus, we could expect them to spread actively the secrets of their immortality among the young, technically developing civilizations.

This optimism with regard to the potential benefits of an encounter with an extraterrestrial civilisation is not shared by all. Ever since [novelist] H.G. Wells' *War of the Worlds*, the sombre image of a threat leading to slavery or the extermination of humanity has been far more widespread in science fiction literature. In his *Profiles of the Future*, Arthur C. Clarke was clearly influenced by that master of imaginative writing, Howard P. Lovecraft, when he wrote: 'The road to Lilliput is short, and it leads nowhere. But the road to Brobdingnag is another matter; we can see along it only a little way, as it winds outwards through the stars, and we cannot guess what strange travellers it carries. It may be well for our peace of mind if we never know.' Fortunately, in his other works, Clarke adopts a much less xenophobic position. At times, he even swings to the opposite extreme, thereby falling into line with Sagan and Drake.

The Controversy Continues

Today the plurality of worlds is a more controversial issue than ever. Arguments on both sides ('It is unlikely that we are alone in the Universe' and 'Where are they?') are of a statistical kind. They are consequently of little import, for statistics cannot be based on the single case provided by life on Earth.

Detection of some inhabited planet, or better still, some extraterrestrial civilisation, would undoubtedly be one of the major landmarks in the history of mankind. On the other hand, non-detection of ETI signals, even after centuries of research, would never prove that there were no extraterrestrial civilisations. But it would be reason to prepare ourselves for a life of cosmic solitude.

SCIENTISTS WONDER WHY NO ALIEN CIVILIZATIONS HAVE BEEN FOUND

NASA Panel Discussion

In 2002 NASA's online *Astrobiology Magazine* published a five-part debate on the question of whether there is intelligent life beyond Earth. Among the scientists who participated were Donald Brownlee, a professor of astronomy at the University of Washington and coauthor of *Rare Earth;* Frank Drake, a professor of astronomy and SETI pioneer who is now chairman of the board of the SETI Institute; David Grinspoon, a principal scientist in the Department of Space Studies at the Southwest Research Institute and author of *Lonely Planets: The Natural Philosophy of Alien Life;* Christopher McKay, a planetary scientist at NASA's Ames Reseach Center; and moderator Michael Meyer, senior scientist for astrobiology at NASA headquarters. In the following portion of the debate, these scientists offer differing opinions about why, if extraterrestrial civilizations exist, astronomers have not yet found any evidence of them.

Michael Meyer: If there is intelligent life out there, why haven't we found them yet?

Christopher McKay: This is Fermi's paradox: Where are they? Or phrased differently: why aren't signs of galactic-scale intelligent life obvious in our telescopes? The simplest explanation for this is that we are the only, or at least the first, intelligent species in the galaxy. Can anyone give a good argument for why our type of civilization would not be obvious over much of the galaxy after a million years?

David Grinspoon: If civilizations like ours were all over the galaxy, it would not be obvious. We are only listening, not broadcasting. We are not doing astroengineering. True, we are leaking sitcoms and beer commercials, but these are not easily detectable over most of the galaxy and certainly would not be interpreted as signs of true intelligence. So, in order to have an obvious presence, "our type of civilization" must become something quite different. Perhaps this is very rare or difficult. However, being a constitutional optimist, and considering the unimaginably vast reaches of time and space, I tend to think that

NASA Panel Discussion, "Great Debates: 'Rare Earth' Part V," *Astrobiology Magazine*, www.astrobio.net, July 29, 2002.

sentient, long-lived civilizations should be out there somewhere. So, where are they?

The reasoning behind Chris's (and Fermi's) question implicitly assumes certain things about the behavior of advanced civilizations. It assumes they will keep expanding their populations and increasing the size of their civil engineering projects. Looking at the history of our civilization and extrapolating to our future, I understand why you could draw such a conclusion. But it may be that truly sentient societies realize there is no future in unlimited expansion. We cannot keep expanding our population at our current rate. Even if we were somehow able to move out into space at the speed of light and colonize all available planets, we would still run out of space and resources and experience mass starvation within a thousand years. True minds will realize that such expansion is a dead end. Of course, the problem with this kind of explanation for "the great silence" (Fermi's paradox) is that it must apply to every single civilization out there. It is hard to believe that every society that ever forms will transform themselves into sustainably living . . . contemplative Buddhists before creating some observable signs of their presence. So, we must search for another answer.

Frank Drake: A parallel question to this is: how long will the Earth's technology be detectable? A few decades ago we thought the visibility would last a long time—ever more powerful TV stations and radar installations were being built, and these are the strongest signs of our existence. But there is only so much bandwidth in the useful electromagnetic spectrum. To transmit ever-increasing amounts of information, portions of the spectrum must be shared. This is only possible if signal strengths are reduced so that transmissions on the same frequency do not interfere with one another. The textbook example of this paradigm is the cellular phone system. This signal reduction means we are well on our way to becoming invisible.

So if the transmission of a rich cornucopia of information is what advanced civilizations do, they may become invisible. This is a rather counter-intuitive result, but a real one. This means that the detectable lifetimes of civilizations may be shorter than we have estimated, and hoped, alas.

They May Not Want to Be Found

David Grinspoon: Another possibility is that they may not want us to know they are there. It's hard for us to fathom the possible motivations and behaviors of societies millions of years older than ours. It seems reasonable, however, to suppose that the differences between their capabilities and ours will be so great that it will be up to them, not us, how and when some kind of detection or contact is made. It is possible that they have decided it should be against the law to let us know they are there (The "Zoo Hypothesis" or the "Prime Directive").

This might be because they are protecting us, studying us, protecting themselves from us or what we might someday become, or waiting until the time is right to initiate us into the Galactic Club.

The simplest explanation—that we are the only, or the at least first, intelligent species in the galaxy—requires an extreme violation of the Copernican Principle (which says the Earth is typical and common). This is especially true when you consider the generations of stars— with possible habitable planets—that lived for billions of years before our star and planet were even a twinkle in the eye in our parent molecular cloud. There has been so much time for someone to come along and achieve intelligence. Why should our present time be so special? It comes down to which unjustified pillar of scientific reasoning you prefer to violate: Occam's Razor (things are simple) or the Copernican Principle (our place is not special). Take your pick.

Interstellar Travel Is Impractical

Frank Drake: Every discussion of alien intelligence assumes that they will come visit us. But the expense and danger of space travel are formidable. A strong reason why such enterprises are not carried out may be that radio communication works so much better, is far cheaper, and you get your answers at the speed of light.

Any reasonable transport of creatures across space calls for travel speeds that are a substantial fraction of the speed of light, otherwise it takes too long to go even to the nearest stars. But this exposes the spacecraft to serious hazards. Probably the most serious is the potential for collision with debris—and we are learning that space is full of debris. At relativistic speeds, even a collision with a particle of a few grams results in something close in energy to a nuclear bomb blast. Not good news for the space travelers.

Also the energy requirements are ridiculous, at least to us. To send a spacecraft the size of a small airliner at one-tenth the speed of light requires as much energy as the US now produces in more than a hundred years. And that just gets you someplace—it doesn't provide for a landing or a return home. To put it another way, it takes 10 million times as much energy to move a small space colony to another star as it takes to establish the same colony in the home system. And there is plenty of room at home. It is easily calculated that the energy of the sun is enough to sustain more than ten thousand billion billion humans. That seems like enough. Why go to the great expense and danger of going to other stars? Truly intelligent life would laugh at the idea. The only ones who might try are the dumb ones, and they don't know how.

Some Civilizations Will Travel Between Stars

David Grinspoon: I agree that, given the time and energy constraints, any intelligent creatures would have to be nuts to attempt interstellar travel. But you would also have to be nuts to attempt to cross the ocean in a rowboat, and people have done that. Why do we need to go one-tenth the speed of light? What's the hurry? So what if travel times are thousands of years? From the perspective of an individual human life at this stage in our evolution, this seems like a long time. But will the galaxy never, ever, anywhere, produce a creature or cultural entity that doesn't find this span of time daunting? Even at these slow speeds, if someone decided to start spreading across the galaxy they would be able to spread across the whole Milky Way in a few hundred million years, tops, which is still short compared to the life of the galaxy.

I also agree that radio communication makes much more sense than any form of interstellar travel for almost any purpose. Except it's still more fun to go to the game than watch it on TV. I doubt we'll ever achieve warp drive or anything that makes interstellar travel so much faster, better, and cheaper that we can visit a new star system with shapely natives every week like [*Star Trek*'s] Captain Kirk. Still, isn't it extreme to declare that no one will ever travel the interstellar distances?

Donald Brownlee: I have always loved space travel in science fiction, but I take a very dim view of the likelihood that we will be able to send people more than just a short distance away. I know that a future without interstellar travel is a minority view, but it is not at all clear that technology could be developed to transport living humans to habitable places beyond our solar system. I think that it is odd that so many people are sure that we will inevitably evolve to a *Star Trek* society, able to zip across the Galaxy like we drive to the next state. Beaming up and all that stuff seems so easy on TV. Our best bet with foreseeable technology is to use antimatter fuel, but even if we could build the hardware it would take all of our planet's energy production for over a century just to make the fuel. Besides, there are additional problems in technology, funding, and human organization. New discoveries involving navigation and maneuvering are required to get to other earthly oases in space on a comfortable and timely basis. Can all the UFOers really be wrong? Time will surely tell.

Advanced Civilizations May Become Immortal

David Grinspoon: As many brilliant thinkers have pointed out, if a civilization survives to a certain point they could easily become immortal. That is, if they learn how to avoid asteroids and other natural disasters, tame any self-destructive instincts and learn to live sustainably, their lifetime effectively becomes the lifetime of the universe. Yes, I know there are nasty things like gamma ray bursts and other hazards we haven't even discovered yet, but we are talking about technology and an understanding of nature, and of self-understanding, that are many millions of years beyond our own. Migrating between stars to stay alive will not be a hurdle for these "old ones." Comparing this idea to *Star Trek* or UFOs is a cheap shot that ignores the serious literature on this topic. If you don't insist on making the trip within the current human life span, there are no huge technical hurdles.

Donald Brownlee: I am sorry that David considered my previous comments about *Star Trek* and UFOs to be a cheap shot, but I really do believe that the difficulty of practical interstellar travel is horrendously underestimated. In my opinion, the public is being bilked by wishful thinkers that like to write books and muse about futures that we would like to believe are our logical destinies. Perhaps I take too much of a hard-nosed and practical view of this, but doing even simple things in space is difficult, unforgiving, and exceedingly expensive. I am aware of the studies of anti-matter rockets, beamed energy, interstellar ram jets, etc., but all of these ideas have severe problems. As I see it, known physics will never deposit living people on Earthlike planets around other stars. Doing so would require "warp speed" and/or harnessing exotic phenomena such as wormholes or zero-point energy. Unless such radical developments occur, mundane ideas such as antimatter rockets will not do the job. We have gone to the moon, we can go to Mars, but that is likely to be the limit that our resources and foreseeable technology will allow. At our current rate of progress, humans may not even make it beyond the International Space Station. Our bounds in space may be as limited as they are on Earth. We have covered the Earth but it seems highly unlikely that we will ever live more than a kilometer above or a few kilometers beneath its surface.

The suggestion that organisms could easily become immortal if they live long enough is intriguing. There are a number of issues here, including whether "immortal" means "relatively immortal" or "actually immortal." Forever is a very long time—I suggest that nothing physical can ever be immortal. Infinite time is something that the universe cannot keep up with unless things like child universes pop up from time to time to refresh the landscape. If things aren't miraculously refreshed, the universe just runs down over long time scales.

According to new information, the expansion of the universe has accelerated. Lawrence Krauss of Case Western University says that an accelerating universe "would be the worst possible universe, both for the quality and quantity of life. All our knowledge, civilization, and culture are destined to be forgotten. There's no long-term future." A most bleak forecast and at the totally opposite end of the spectrum from predictions of immortal beings.

Advanced Civilizations Must Be Accumulating

David Grinspoon: I define "immortal" as lasting for the rest of the life of the universe, which may not be "really immortal" but may have to do. If we accept the idea that *some* civilizations can solve the problems which threaten their survival, attain peace, stability, control their populations, learn to intelligently engineer their solar systems, etc., then "immortality" happens. By definition it is an irreversible transition, so the immortals must slowly be accumulating. None of us know, but my sense is that the universe is bio-friendly. I doubt there are any other planets with a peculiar history and biosphere closely resembling Earth's, but I predict many, many inhabited worlds, and a large number with intelligence far in advance of anything we can even conceive of. Don't you love predictions like this? It cannot be proven wrong!

ALIEN ARTIFACTS MAY HAVE FALLEN TO EARTH

Marcus Chown

Marcus Chown, formerly a radio astronomer at the California Institute of Technology in Pasadena, is now cosmology consultant of the British weekly science magazine *New Scientist*. He lives in London. Chown has written three popular science books as well as a children's book on astronomy, and he has coauthored two science fiction novels. In the following selection he explains why Ukrainian astrophysicist Alexey Arkhipov believes it's likely that alien "space junk" from other solar systems floats between the stars. According to Arkhipov, enough of this alien trash may have fallen to Earth in the past to be worth searching for.

In the movie *2001: A Space Odyssey*, an alien artifact is dug up on the Moon. Exposed to the light of the lunar dawn for the first time in millions of years, it promptly broadcasts a message to the stars: "I've been found!" Long ago, when its extraterrestrial makers swept through the solar system, they observed the abundant life on the third planet from the Sun and recognized its potential. They could not stop with so many other stars to explore. However, they buried a "sentinel" on the Moon, a kind of burglar alarm to warn them if one day intelligence arose on the third planet, sidestepped nuclear annihilation, and ventured out of its cradle into space.

Is it likely that there really are alien artifacts buried beneath the surface of the Moon, or even the surface of Earth? The astonishing answer, says Alexey Arkhipov of the Institute of Radio Astronomy in Kharkov, is yes. If intelligent life elsewhere in our galaxy has arisen and made the leap into space, the presence of alien artifacts on our cosmic doorstep is not only likely but guaranteed.

The claim, at first sight, seems utterly mad. However, it is important to understand what is and isn't being claimed by Arkhipov. He is not claiming that alien artifacts have been left on Earth deliberately, as they were on the Moon in *2001*. That would require intention, and who are we to guess the intentions of an extraterrestrial civilization,

Marcus Chown, *The Universe Next Door: The Making of Tomorrow's Science*. New York: Oxford University Press, 2002. Copyright © 2002 by Marcus Chown. Reproduced by permission of Oxford University Press, Inc.

far in advance of our own? No, the alien artifacts Arkhipov is actually referring to are ones that have fallen to Earth accidentally.

How could artifacts get here accidentally? For an answer, says Arkhipov, we need look no farther than our own cosmic backyard. Human activities in space "pollute" our solar system. Agencies in the space business have become increasingly alarmed by the accumulation in space of dead satellites, discarded rocket casings, and the like. This "space junk" clutters Earth's orbit and is so hazardous to space traffic that it has already led to the postponing of more than one launch of NASA's space shuttle.

But—and this is Arkhipov's point—interplanetary garbage does not stay interplanetary garbage forever. It is inevitable that, over time, some man-made artifacts will actually leave the solar system. Buffeted by the winds of space, they will sail off toward the stars.

Escape from the Solar System

Several distinct processes can eject debris from the solar system, according to Arkhipov. First, there is the pressure of sunlight. Sunlight is actually a wind of tiny particles known as photons, which flood out from the Sun in their countless quadrillions. We are not directly aware of this wind from the Sun because it is so weak. Nevertheless, it can sweep a body clean out of the solar system—if the body is small enough.

The reason size matters is that to break free of the Sun's powerful gravity, a body must attain an "escape velocity" of more than 600 kilometers per second, or 1.38 million miles per hour. Because the wind from the Sun is so weak, the only bodies that it can accelerate to this speed are very small—no more than a thousandth of a millimeter across. This happens to be the typical size of particles blasted from rocket exhausts. Such particles can be picked up by the photon breeze and blown past the outermost planets and out into the void beyond.

Bigger bits of debris can also be boosted to the high speed necessary to escape the solar system. According to Arkhipov, this can happen if they collide with each other in space or if they spontaneously explode. In recent years, several planetary space probes are thought to have been destroyed when they either collided with meteorites in space or spontaneously exploded. According to Arkhipov, if such a collision or explosion were to occur in the outer part of the solar system, where the grip of the Sun's gravity is weak, chunks of high-speed debris could be jettisoned into interstellar space.

There is a third means of expelling space debris from the solar system in addition to sunlight pressure and collisions/explosions. This is the close encounter of an artifact with a planet. In such an encounter, known as a "gravitational slingshot," the gravity of the planet actually catapults the artifact into interstellar space. Computer simulations have shown that, over time, more than a third of the minor planets, or "asteroids," will be ejected from the solar system in this manner.

Space Junk from the Stars

Arkhipov's reason for highlighting the mechanisms by which debris can be ejected into interstellar space is to point out that they could just as well act in reverse. In the same way that human activities pollute the solar system with garbage, the activities of any space-faring extraterrestrials will similarly fill their planetary system with space junk. And, just as our technological activities lead to the spread of artifacts into interstellar space, so too will theirs. The consequences of this, says Arkhipov, are obvious. "If alien artifacts are really floating between the stars," he says, "some of them will inevitably fall to Earth."

Arkhipov's reasoning is based on the absolute inevitability of accidents in space. His only assumption is that our galaxy does indeed contain other space-faring societies. If it doesn't, then his argument is void. But then so too is the argument for SETI, the much-publicized search for extraterrestrial intelligence, which currently involves radio and optical astronomers scanning the heavens in the hope of picking up an intelligent message from the stars. "For Christopher Columbus, the evidence of new lands was strange debris which had floated across the ocean," says Arkhipov. "In the same way, debris which has floated across the ocean of space could provide us with the unmistakable evidence of new planets and new life."

Assuming that there are other space-faring societies in the Milky Way, Arkhipov then poses the following extraordinary question: "During its four-and-a-half-billion-year history, how many alien artifacts could have fallen to Earth?"

How Many Alien Artifacts?

The answer depends on a number of factors. Say each alien civilization in our galaxy has at its disposal the same amount of material as exists in our own asteroid belt. This amounts to roughly 1.8 trillion trillion grams. Now assume that each civilization over the course of its history transforms 1 percent of that material into technological artifacts. This may seem a lot. However, on Earth we are used to an "exponential" growth in the amount of material we can process—a doubling in a certain period, then doubling again and again. If this kind of increase were to continue once an alien civilization became space faring, says Arkhipov, the civilization might plausibly process 1 percent of its asteroidal material into the extraterrestrial equivalent of consumer goods in just a few million years.

Now for the numbers. One percent of 1.8 billion trillion grams is 18 billion trillion grams. If this amount of asteroidal material is converted into objects of, say, mass 100 grams—the size of a pepper shaker—this comes to 180 billion billion artifacts.

Not every star has a family of planets, although it appears from recent observations of nearby stars that as many as 30 percent do. And not every planetary system is likely to spawn a space-faring civilization that makes interstellar artifacts. But say, just for the sake of argument, 1 percent of civilizations do. How common will alien artifacts then be?

Inserting the figures, the answer is that every cube of space with sides 130 million kilometers long should have one artifact floating in it. This is a truly enormous volume—roughly the distance of Earth from the Sun. Searching for an alien artifact the size of a pepper shaker in this much empty space makes hunting down the proverbial needle in a haystack child's play. From the cosmic perspective, however, alien artifacts would be surprisingly common.

Imagine, then, that the whole of space, stretching out to the most distant stars, is divided into cubes 130 million kilometers on a side and that, drifting somewhere in each cube, is one alien artifact. Now, the Sun is not sitting still. It is flying through space with Earth and planets in tow. As it does so, it is therefore flying through a cloud of alien artifacts. It's rather like someone running through a cloud of mosquitoes—except that the cloud of alien artifacts is considerably more rarefied than any conceivable cloud of mosquitoes. The question Arkhipov asks is: how often will Earth run into an alien artifact?

How Many May Fall to Earth?

Crudely speaking, any artifact that happens to fly through the space between Earth and the Sun will stand a chance of running into Earth. Think of the space inside Earth's orbit as a circular target flying through a swarm of mosquitoes. Actually, the target can appear bigger than Earth's orbit because the gravity of the Sun can pull in passing artifacts even if they pass farther out from the Sun than Earth. It all depends on their speed. If an artifact races through the solar system at high velocity, it will have to come within Earth's orbit in order to hit Earth. If, however, it drifts slowly through the solar system, it can be snared from farther afield.

How fast will these artifacts be moving? Well, they come from the stars, and the Sun is moving relative to the nearby stars, and these stars in turn have a spread of velocities. Arkhipov calculates that because of this motion, we can expect a piece of space garbage to come at us at about 32 kilometers per second on average, or 115,000 kilometers per hour.

At this point, we have almost everything we need in order to calculate how often Earth runs into an alien artifact. We know the size of the target that the space inside Earth's orbit presents to mosquito-like artifacts. We have an estimate of how common such artifacts are throughout space. And we know how fast the Earth-Sun target is flying through the cloud of artifacts.

As the target travels through space, it "sweeps out" a cylindrical volume of space. Any artifact that happens to be in that cylinder can potentially fall to Earth. To fall to Earth, it must actually run smack bang into Earth, and Earth presents an even smaller target than the space within Earth's orbit. However, taking this into consideration as well, Arkhipov finally answers the question: how many hundred-gram alien artifacts have fallen to Earth in its 4.6 billion-year history? The answer, incredible as it sounds, is four thousand.

It's an amazing figure. But it applies only if the underlying assumptions are correct. In other words, if 1 percent of the planetary system spawns a space-faring civilization that turns an amount of material equivalent to 1 percent of the asteroid belt into hundred-gram artifacts.

Alien Garbage May Be Here

The numbers are, of course, flexible. For instance, it could be that only one in ten thousand planetary systems produces a space-faring civilization during its lifetime. This would mean revising down the number of alien artifacts on Earth to a mere forty. Not a lot, perhaps. But emphatically not zero. Or say space-faring civilizations transform a smaller mass of material into artifacts or transform the mass into bigger artifacts. Well, in both cases, the figure of four thousand will need to be scaled down. But the amazing thing is that it has to be scaled down by a factor of more than four thousand to be less than one.

Arkhipov's extraordinary conclusion is that if a reasonable proportion of planetary systems produces space-faring extraterrestrials, then alien garbage must exist on Earth. This assumes that such material does not burn up completely as it plunges down through the atmosphere. However, Arkhipov believes that moderate-sized artifacts have a good chance of surviving this ordeal by fire, at least in part.

The evidence of extraterrestrials, according to Arkhipov, could literally be beneath our feet. Consequently, scientists should seriously consider looking for alien artifacts in geological strata and among unusual meteorites. "The discovery of ET evidence seems possible not only in the sky but on Earth as well!" he says.

Comparisons can be made with SETI, the search for extraterrestrial intelligence. Whereas our radio dishes have presented a target for alien radio traffic for little more than forty years, Earth, and especially the Moon, have been sitting targets for alien garbage for more than four billion years. That's one hundred million times longer. Moreover, a basic assumption of SETI is that extraterrestrials not only possess a desire to communicate but that they use a means—radio or optical signals—that we at our present stage of advancement are able to recognize. By contrast, the mere existence of extraterrestrials is enough to guarantee that their garbage eventually falls onto Earth and the Moon. "The search for alien space debris is the missed chance of modern science," says Arkhipov.

Where to Look for Alien Artifacts

Probably the best place to look for alien artifacts is on the Moon, as Arthur Clarke guessed. The Moon, after all, has not been weathered or remade by geological forces apart from meteorite impacts. "The lunar surface must be studied by archaeologists," says Arkhipov.

The Moon, however, is beyond our reach at present and our best bet is our own planet. The first thing to say is that almost two-thirds of Earth is ocean. It follows that this is the most likely place for an alien artifact to come down. The pressure at the foot of the deepest ocean trenches is cripplingly high and we cannot go there, but must send our robotic emissaries instead. As oceanographers are fond of saying, the bed of the ocean is less well known than the surface of the Moon. It does not bode too well for finding the odd alien artifact the size of a pepper shaker.

So much for the oceans. What of Earth's dry land? This must contend with the remorseless effect of wind, rain, and ice, which over time can weather away even the tallest mountains. But even these forces pale into insignificance beside the geological ones that, over hundreds of millions of millions of years, have seen new oceans open up and continents dive into oblivion in the magma beneath our feet. The prospects for an alien artifact falling to Earth do not look good. In fact, any artifact that fell to Earth more than a billion years ago has probably long ago been dragged down into Earth, crushed, and transformed by the heat and pressure of the planet's interior.

However, it may be that few alien artifacts fell to Earth in the first few billion years of its history. There is a hidden assumption in Arkhipov's reasoning and that is that space-faring civilizations have always been around. It turns out, however, that the heavy atoms necessary for life, such as carbon and oxygen and iron, are baked inside the ovens of stars before being spewed into space to be incorporated into new stars. This process ensures that successive generations of stars have been richer in heavy elements and it may be that a certain threshold level of heavy atoms is needed before life-bearing planets like Earth are possible. Consequently, Earth could be one of the first, and intelligent life might not have arisen elsewhere long before it did on Earth.

For a number of reasons, therefore, any artifacts we might find would be likely to be from the last billion years. How then would we recognize one? It stands to reason that we are unlikely to find an alien transistor radio in rocks containing dinosaur bones.

Would Artifacts Be Recognized?

Here we have a major problem. Would people from the nineteenth century recognize a silicon chip? Would they realize that it was an artifact of an advanced technological civilization? Would they realize that it could carry out millions, or even billions, of calculations a second? Nineteenth-century chemists might conclude that the chip was made of an element called silicon and that there were traces of other elements such as gold. But they would be unlikely to guess its purpose. The situation would be even worse if the chip had lain around for years so that it was weathered and eroded.

And here we are talking of a span of only a hundred years. An advanced extraterrestrial civilization might be thousands, even millions, of years ahead of us. Its artifacts might be as unrecognizable to us as a dishwasher is to an ant, or even an amoeba. In the words of [science fiction author] Arthur C. Clarke: "Any technology that is sufficiently advanced is indistinguishable from magic."

Our only hope, it would seem, would be to find a puzzling piece of rock or metal with an unusual chemical composition or even an unusual nuclear composition.

Somewhere in the world a puzzling artifact is lying in a museum. Perhaps nobody has noticed it for a century or more. Or perhaps, at this very moment, a curator is taking it out of a glass case, looking at it, and scratching his or her head in bafflement. Will the curator take it to be chemically analyzed? Or will the curator put it back in the case and forget about it forever? We can only hope that doesn't happen.

CHAPTER 3

HAVE EXTRATERRESTRIALS VISITED EARTH?

Contemporary Issues
Companion

ALIENS WOULD VISIT AND OBSERVE, NOT SEND SIGNALS

Terence Dickinson

Terence Dickinson has written fifteen books on astronomy and is editor of the Canadian magazine *Sky News*. The following selection is from the newest edition of his classic astronomy book *The Universe and Beyond*. In it, he explains why he thinks extraterrestrials would visit other worlds instead of sending radio messages to them. SETI has been based on the assumption that interstellar travel would be too expensive, but that assumption does not take into account technological advances now envisioned, let alone those that might be made by a much older alien civilization. Dickinson believes that although there is no evidence of their presence, it is likely that extraterrestrials are passively observing Earth at a critical point in human history.

The newspaper cartoon strip *Frank & Ernest* sometimes features a pair of curious aliens scouting Earth in a flying saucer. One such excursion involved a decision about where to land. Finally, Alien A says to Alien B (they both look like humanoid dogs with antennas), "Land in New York or southern California so we won't look too conspicuous."

Apart from its regional earthbound jibe, the comic strip repeats once more the implicit assumption made by countless cartoonists, science fiction writers and movie producers that aliens are indeed in the Earth's vicinity considering how to make contact with us dumb Earthlings. Judging by the box-office receipts of films ranging from *Independence Day* to *Close Encounters of the Third Kind*, the idea has enormous popular appeal. But scientific opinion has been generally negative, with few outright advocates of the they-are-nearby-and-watching-us school.

I believe the objections to this popular notion are based more on emotional than scientific grounds, because recent findings in such diverse fields as astrophysics, biology, computer technology, planetary geology and spacecraft propulsion technology all support it in various ways. I also feel that one of the least plausible scenarios is that of creatures' signaling us with radio transmitters from a planet of a nearby star. It seems to me far more likely that such random contact is the last thing alien intelligences would want to achieve. . . .

Interstellar Travel

That we are exploring other planets and moons in our own solar system places us at a pivotal evolutionary juncture which sentient creatures on other worlds either passed long ago or have not yet reached. The technological advancement from steam engine to computer over the past two centuries took but a metaphorical fraction of a second in the life of the universe. The swiftness of technological progress that we witness during a single human lifetime means the odds must be heavily stacked against two civilizations in a galaxy being anywhere close to the same technological century. As the late [astronomer] Carl Sagan once said, "To us, they would be either gods or brutes." Societies that evolved before us would regard the discovery of interstellar travel as ancient history.

Given time and the appropriate technology, there is no reason extraterrestrials could not travel around the galaxy or beyond. Lengthy interstellar voyages could be achieved by retarding the biological clock that controls the aging process, by making the ship large enough to accommodate a microcosm of civilization, by sending surrogates in the form of robots or by avoiding the time factor altogether by traveling very close to the speed of light to utilize the time-dilation effect. Fusion or matter-antimatter propulsion systems could tap virtually limitless energy sources, permitting unbounded exploration.

But after space travel becomes commonplace and problems of health and energy abundance are solved, one question would remain for any curious civilization. Does the universe harbor other rational creatures? Unless advanced civilizations are spread so thinly that there are fewer than one per galaxy, they will become aware of each other sooner or later. Either individually or collectively, the civilizations which arose before us in our galaxy must have thoroughly surveyed their interstellar environment, if for no other reason than to attempt to answer that question. Long ago, the process would have led to the discovery of life on Earth.

Despite the fact that our planet is a relative newcomer on the galactic timescale, the oceans have nurtured life-forms for three billion years, about one-fifth of the age of the galaxy—ample time for Earth to have been noticed as a life-bearing world. This may sound like the background for a science fiction movie, but consider the alternatives: If aliens are not aware of us, they must have all self-destructed or they are not interested or we have always been alone or they are there but have not yet discovered us. . . .

The final alternative assumes that no other civilizations explore beyond their local neighborhood. Supporters of this view argue that interstellar travel is technologically difficult and enormously expensive and that consequently, it would not be commonly done. I have always thought that such arguments express "difficulty" and "expense" in terms of 20th-century or, at best, 21st-century technologies. Even the most perceptive visionaries, such as H.G. Wells and Leonardo da Vinci, projected technological progress only a few centuries. No one alive today can possibly guess what devices will propel us—or our consciousness—to the stars. In principle, interstellar travel does not defy the laws of physics. Or as noted science fiction author Arthur C. Clarke has said: "Any sufficiently advanced technology will seem to us like magic."

The Quest for Signals

Interstellar travel is the most direct way to seek life on other worlds. Nothing can equal actually taking a close look. And firsthand investigation is probably the only way that creatures less technologically developed than humans could be detected. Searching for alien signals with radio telescopes will yield results only if other civilizations are staying at home making long-distance calls to their galactic relatives via radio frequencies. Radio-search advocates not only admit this but have enshrined the concept in what Princeton University physicist Freeman Dyson calls "a philosophical discourse dogma." He says the radio searchers assume "as an article of faith" that higher civilizations communicate by radio in preference to all other options.

Prior to 1959, there was no dogma on the search for intelligent extraterrestrials. All references to the subject were found only between the covers of science fiction books and magazines, where interstellar spaceships were an integral part of the picture. Then, almost overnight, everything changed. It became scientifically respectable (or, in the view of some, tolerable) to talk about contacting aliens because the prestigious journal *Nature* published an article by physicists Philip Morrison and Giuseppe Cocconi describing the relative ease of transmitting radio signals across the galaxy and how it might be possible, using radio telescopes, to detect such signals from other intelligences. Hundreds of articles and dozens of books embellishing the concept have appeared since this watershed article, but the basic idea has remained constant.

The first actual search, by astronomer Frank Drake, was conducted a few months after the Morrison-Cocconi article was published. Along with Cornell University's Carl Sagan, Drake went on to become the subject's most visible spokesman. Recognizing that interstellar spaceships and radio searches are concepts in conflict, Drake advanced the often-repeated argument of the extreme difficulties and the enormous expense involved in interstellar travel. But that was in the early 1960s. Since then, dozens of serious research reports and proposals have detailed various interstellar propulsion systems that are considered reasonable extrapolations of late-20th century technology. That weakened the rationale for the radio searches, and by the mid-1970s, a significant number of astronomers were calling for a reassessment of the assumptions. In the ensuing discussions in scientific journals, those interested in the question split into two camps: the agnostics and the dogmatists. Scientists from one group are seldom invited to SETI (search for extraterrestrial intelligence) conferences organized by the other.

The Search Strategy's Assumptions

Radio search advocates have one powerful comeback: If we do not listen, we will never know for sure. I do not object to someone's monitoring the cosmic radio dial; however, the public's perception of the activity is that researchers are attempting to eavesdrop on alien conversations, which is not what the radio quest is all about. Even if the galaxy were humming with alien radio communications, we almost certainly would not intercept any of them unless the transmissions were outrageously extravagant in signal power, which goes against the initial argument about the efficiency of radio communication. Signals directed from point A to point B in the galaxy would be undetectable unless we happened to be precisely between the two points— an enormous improbability. Our radio telescopes are far too weak to pick up conversations not focused in our direction.

Could we recognize other kinds of signals? Earthlings have broadcast their existence for about 70 years through radio, television, radar and other electronic transmissions that escape into space. This "noise" floods out from our planet at the speed of light and now forms an expanding bubble of babble 70 light-years in radius. But could we detect the noise from another civilization? According to a 1970 study conducted by Woodruff T. Sullivan and his colleagues at the University of Washington, existing equipment would be able to pick up electronic "leakage" of television- and radar-type emissions from only a few dozen light-years away—a radius that includes fewer than 200 stars. In the decades since that study, the sensitivity of our receivers has advanced to extend the detection radius to include thousands of stars, but this affords us little advantage, because electronic leakage from an Earthlike planet would be swamped within a few hundred light-years by the static of natural cosmic radio sources.

In any case, such leakage would not last for long, according to Sagan. "I think there is just a 100-year spike in radio emissions before a planet becomes radio-quiet again," he said in a published interview in the 1980s. He pointed out that communications on Earth are rapidly moving from brute-force broadcasting to narrow-beam transmission satellite dishes, fiber optics and cable television—all of which are relatively low power. Sagan's assessment: "the chance of success in eavesdropping is negligible."

Despite the frequent use of the word "eavesdropping" in connection with the SETI programs, most of the searches have been limited almost entirely to finding either a superpowerful omnidirectional beacon or a narrow-beam signal intentionally directed toward us. Such a search strategy therefore assumes that extraterrestrials either know about us or are pumping a colossal signal in all directions in the hope that somebody is listening.

A number of thorny questions emerge from all of this. How long would a civilization continue to broadcast an omnidirectional signal? Since it would take hundreds of thousands of years for a response, would everybody be listening and no one sending? And why would an alien civilization want to broadcast, not knowing who would intercept the message, what culture shock it would cause or who might be around on their home planet to receive a reply centuries or millennia in the future? If a signal is intentionally beamed in our direction, the senders must know we are here. Is the universe so perverse in its structure that it constricts intelligences to a destiny of exploration by megaphone? Is it possible that extraterrestrials might consider radio transmission to be as quaint as we regard smoke signals or jungle drums? . . .

Wishful Thinking?

In 1978, at the height of scientific interest in the radio searches, Sagan wrote his most optimistic article on the quest for an intentional signal from another civilization. "Since the transmission is likely to be from a civilization far in advance of our own," he wrote in *Reader's Digest*, "stunning insights are possible, [including] prescriptions for the avoidance of technological disaster. Perhaps it will describe which pathways of cultural evolution are likely to lead to the stability and longevity of intelligent species. Or perhaps there are straightforward solutions, still undiscovered on Earth, to problems of food shortage, population growth, energy supplies, dwindling resources, pollution and war."

And Sagan was not the only one to express such a view. Frankly, I think suggestions that messages from aliens will solve all our problems not only are presumptuous but also smack more of religion than science. Surely superior intelligences in the universe have graduated to something more creative than operating broadcasting stations to send galactic versions of the Ten Commandments to the heathens.

Our own experience on this planet suggests that contact between technologically imbalanced cultures is bad news for the number-two culture. Painful assimilation and cultural decimation seem to be the products of such contact, even with the best of intentions. Maybe there is some biogalactic law among advanced civilizations that forbids direct intervention with primitives like us. In any event, technologically superior intelligences could probably make themselves completely undetectable, leisurely learning all they care to know about life on Earth without our being aware of the scrutiny.

Their physical appearance may also be unrecognizable to us. They may once have passed through an evolutionary phase when they resembled humans, but the lizard men and the gaggle of other humanoids from the *Star Wars* and *Star Trek* movies are probably not who (or what) we will meet. Evolution beyond humanlike form is as inevitable as our ascent from our reptilian ancestors. One billion years ago, the highest from of life on Earth was the worm. An alien intelligence one billion years ahead of us on the evolutionary ladder could be as different from us as we are from worms. . . .

Perhaps bodies of bone and flesh are already redundant in the universe, and advanced civilizations have become virtually indestructible semi-immortal arrays of silicon or its evolutionary successor. To such a form of intelligence, time would have a totally different meaning. With no finite life span to impede time-consuming activities such as interstellar travel, millions of years could be spent in exploration. Voyages to countless star systems would present no problems for a semi-immortal brain. To such travelers, emerging intelligences like ours would be fascinating biological crucibles. Occasionally, they might look in on Earth to glimpse the latest tribal squabble and wonder when we will emerge to seek our place in the galactic community.

What About UFOs?

If aliens can travel here, then where are they? Where are their artifacts, their spaceships, their supply bases? So far, there is not a shred of hard evidence that extraterrestrials exist, either in our vicinity or in deep space. But absence of evidence is not evidence of absence. A century ago, it would have been impossible to identify a modern reconnaissance satellite—able to spot a human shadow in a playing field from an altitude of 200 kilometers—as anything more than a mysterious moving dot of light tracking across the night sky. Even that could be concealed by coating the spacecraft in ultralow-reflective material. Because there could be millions of years of technical advancement between Earthlings and aliens, it might be a simple matter for them to remain undetected. Yet thousands of reports of strange aerial phenomena—unidentified flying objects, or UFOs—have been cited as proof that extraterrestrial devices are exploring Earth.

I delved seriously into the subject after I saw a UFO in 1973 that was witnessed by 18 other people. I was teaching a class in astronomy at a planetarium in Rochester, New York. We were outside identifying constellations when we saw a formation of lights pass silently almost overhead, then veer off and swoop toward the horizon. It is not impossible for an aircraft or a group of aircraft to behave in this manner, but I had never seen that kind of formation nor the type of lights we observed.

What made the sighting even more baffling was being told when I called the air force base responsible for the local airspace that no military vehicles were anywhere near the area at the time in question. A controller at the local airport said the same thing. Only through persistent sleuthing did I finally discover that what we had seen was, in fact, a small fleet of experimental military aircraft with high-intensity downfacing lights, apparently top secret at the time.

If I had been unable to take the time and effort to research the case properly, I would have been left with a lifelong UFO story to tell. That is not to say every UFO which has ever been seen can be explained in a conventional manner, as some debunkers would have us believe. A small number of cases have been thoroughly investigated and remain a mystery. These may represent a hitherto undiscovered phenomenon, perhaps a rare atmospheric electro-magnetic effect. Extraterrestrial spaceships capture the imagination because they are the most dramatic of the possibilities.

Some accounts of UFO and flying-saucer sightings have become modern legends. They include explicit descriptions of alien creatures and, in a few cases, bizarre tales of aliens that allegedly abducted humans for hours or days. I became sufficiently intrigued by such reports that I interviewed some of the "abductees." Despite the sincerity of these people, I remain unconvinced—and I was ready to be convinced. I have no bias against the ability of extraterrestrials to traverse the gulfs between the stars to explore Earth, but there are too many inconsistencies. Why, for instance, would they allow themselves to be seen as UFOs—elusive, yet hinting at so much—playing peekaboo with the natives? Are we to conclude that aliens choosing to venture close to Earth are *almost* clever enough to go undetected, but not quite? I think not.

Over the years, I have investigated many UFO sightings and was, for a time, a consultant for a major scientific UFO study, which forced me to give serious thought to the matter. I have concluded that the investigation of UFOs is not a fruitful avenue to pursue in the hopes of contacting our cosmic cousins, although it may prove of value in some other way.

In the late 1960s and early 1970s, discussions of UFOs entered the pages of scientific journals and engaged the interest of a cross section of researchers ranging from astronomers to psychologists. But that era seems to have ended, and UFOs have virtually disappeared from the pages of scientific publications.

Why Earth Would Interest Aliens

The standard science fiction stories of aliens invading Earth represent, in my view, the least likely scenario. Cultures more advanced than ours will be benign; they will have learned to live with themselves. Aggressive creatures prone to squabbling and warfare would be weeded out by natural selection—they would destroy themselves. If by some fluke they did not, they would be kept in check by even more advanced civilizations acting as galactic police. Otherwise, we would have known about them by now, because creatures with the will and the power to enslave or destroy us would have done so long ago.

We may be a celestial nature sanctuary that has reached a critical evolutionary stage. For the first time, the specter of self-annihilation looms as a possibility. We would be of prime interest to alien intelligences. To understand why, consider the opposite point of view. When we have the ability to travel to solar systems beyond our own, the most exquisite discovery we could make would be other living creatures. Even recognizing a lowly bacterium on another world will be a momentous event, telling us at last that we are not alone. But that revelation would pale in comparison with the detection of a world harboring creatures which might eventually evolve to contemplate their own existence. In any conceivable circumstance, thoughts of conquest or destruction of such a crucible would be totally pointless.

The most valuable thing we Earthlings have to offer advanced aliens is ourselves in our natural state. We are a biological and scientific oasis, a living example of intelligent beings climbing the evolutionary ladder. We are at the crucial stage where we will either become spacefaring creatures or plunge ourselves into a catastrophe of our own making. Whatever the outcome, I believe our cosmic relatives are likely aware of us and are observing our progress with interest.

Passive observation and nonintervention are the only approaches that would pay reasonable dividends for extraterrestrials. Despite efforts to eavesdrop on extraterrestrials with radio telescopes, the odds favor the belief that the aliens already know about us and are silent observers. We will remain unaware of them until they are ready to talk. Contact will be made at a time and in a manner of their choosing, not ours.

IT IS LIKELY THAT SOME UFOS ARE EXTRATERRESTRIAL

Don Berliner

Don Berliner is chairman of the Fund for UFO Research (FUFOR), a nonprofit organization that aims to support scientific efforts to learn the nature of the UFO phenomenon. He is the author of many books and articles on aviation history and sports aviation. In the following selection he summarizes the evidence for the existence of UFOs that cannot be explained away as natural phenomena or mistaken sightings of civilian or military aircraft. Berliner's conclusion is that because of recent discoveries in astrobiology, it seems increasingly likely that some UFOs are of extraterrestrial origin.

About the only point that can be made concerning UFOs without the risk of starting an unpleasant controversy is that they are supremely controversial. Any discussion of their nature, their origins, their significance and, indeed, their very existence, has led to long-term arguments that have yet to reach any generally agreed-upon conclusion.

On the pivotal questions of their being real and of a novel nature, the reasons employed by the negative side focus on the lack of scientifically acceptable proof of the presence of a single UFO. Expert testimony, photographs and radar trackings are discounted as insufficiently scientific. And since UFOs are so often equated with extraterrestrial spacecraft, the negative side points to the alleged impossibility of, and the lack of motivation for, traveling astronomical distances for undetermined purposes.

Those on the positive side point to the same evidence and suggest that comparable material and equally qualified witnesses are accepted by the legal systems of most countries. As for the possibility that UFOs are extraterrestrial spacecraft (a leap that is not necessarily justified), pro-UFO activists say that any discussion of the likelihood of travel from other possible worlds depends on unavailable knowledge of the technology of those operating UFOs, their normal life spans and their motivations (or lack of same) for traveling extreme distances.

The Evidence

Evidence of a UFO sighting may be anecdotal (the description of a personal experience) and/or recorded (photographic, radar, physical). The reliability of any anecdote depends on the amount and precision of the data, and the personal character and technical background of the witness(es). The usefulness of reliable data depends on its nature: Does it point to a conventional explanation or toward something unconventional?

If every UFO report could be convincingly credited to some conventional astronomical or atmospheric phenomenon, there would be no UFO mystery. It is precisely because so many UFO reports *cannot* logically be blamed on stars, planets, satellites, airplanes, balloons, etc., that a UFO mystery has existed since at least the mid-1940s.

The most convincing UFO reports were produced in the 1940s, 1950s and 1960s by airline pilots, military pilots and ex-military pilots. These men had the training and the experience to be able to distinguish between normal sky sights and highly abnormal sights. They knew what airplanes looked like, and what meteors looked like, having seen them many times. Their visual observations were frequently supported by radar data which showed essentially the same thing. They were therefore able, on many occasions, to methodically eliminate conventional phenomena from consideration when trying to identify UFOs.

In those same decades, most UFO sightings were made in the daytime and frequently at close range, when shapes and surface features could be distinguished, thus making positive identification of normal sights easier and the descriptions of unusual sights more detailed. When all normal explanations had been eliminated, the witnesses could concentrate on those aspects of the experience which were most abnormal.

These abnormal aspects included the shapes of UFOs and their behavior. Most of the UFOs seen in the daytime were said to have had simple geometric shapes—discs, ovals, spheres, cylinders—and surfaces that looked like metal. Such shapes are not only nonexistent among known aircraft, but contrary to all known theories of flight, in most cases offering control and performance disadvantages rather than advantages.

Even more unusual were the specifics of their flight performance: silent hovering, silent high-speed flight, extreme acceleration, supersonic flight at low altitude without sonic booms, and violent, very high-g maneuvers. The actions of many UFOs have suggested that they fly independently of the air and even of the force of gravity. The accomplishment of these maneuvers has been among the major goals of the world's aerospace industry for decades.

On the basis of their appearance, behavior and frequent well-kept, tight formation flights, we must face the possibility that some UFOs may be manufactured, high-tech vehicles. If this is the case, they must be either ours or someone else's. Any "UFOs" that are ours should be well known to the U.S. military, which would have been eager to so label them and remove them from the embarrassing "unidentified" category.

Secret American Aircraft?

While there are always some military aircraft that are being kept secret for perfectly good reasons, the classified status of their appearance, at least, is generally changed as soon as they become operational or are declared unsuccessful and thus obsolete. It is possible that currently secret American aircraft may display one or more characteristics generally attributed to UFOs, but those listed as secret in the 1940s, 1950s and 1960s can reasonably be assumed to be familiar to aviation experts, if not to every member of the general public. They have either gone into production or have been consigned to the scrap heap or to museums.

If we acknowledge the extremely unlikely chance that highly advanced American military weapons have been kept secret for three or more decades—something not known to have happened at any time in history—we must face the very serious implications. We must have spent hundreds of billions of dollars on known and highly inferior aircraft to be used in a cover-up of such deeply classified activities. These inferior aircraft must have been used and continue to be used while far superior aircraft have been kept in hiding instead of being employed to prevent or win wars which have cost many lives and endangered many more.

Such actions would be unprecedented and indefensible. If a country possesses superior aircraft, it does not equip several generations of its air force with second-rate equipment. It does not throw such inferior aircraft into combat when it has quantities of superior aircraft that would stand a far better chance of winning battles quickly and more certainly. It therefore seems extremely unlikely that most of the unidentifiable UFOs seen 30 or more years ago could be American military aircraft. They must, therefore, be foreign.

Secret Foreign Aircraft?

The presence in American skies of aircraft from friendly foreign nations such as Canada, Great Britain, France and Israel would be known to American military authorities and would almost certainly be known to the civilian (FAA) air traffic control system. If there have been considerable numbers of superior foreign aircraft flying over the USA since World War II, they must have been here for good reasons known to the American military. But these countries have also experienced large numbers of puzzling UFO reports, and therefore are in the same uncomfortable position as the USA.

If, by any chance, one or more friendly nations had created such greatly superior aircraft, the U.S. military would almost certainly have purchased them or had them produced here under license, as has been done with the English Electric Canberra jet bomber and the British Aerospace Corp. Harrier VTOL fighter. As with American-built superior aircraft, these would not be kept secret for decades, and would not have been held in reserve when they were needed for defense or combat.

The likelihood of highly advanced aircraft from less-than-friendly nations flying for decades over the USA without permission or notification is even smaller than the likelihood of friendly foreign aircraft doing so. In this case, there would be the additional great risk of accidental war upon their discovery and identification, and the only slightly lesser risk of the loss of priceless advanced technology in case of a crash or forced landing.

The only unfriendly nation that could have developed and then produced even slightly advanced aircraft would have been the USSR. Other unfriendly nations, such as Communist China, Libya, Iran, Iraq and Cuba, were even more lacking than was the USSR in the intellectual and industrial capability needed to achieve massive technological breakthroughs. Any of these nations—or other nations—would, of course, have repeatedly made use of such superior weapons to achieve political and economic ends which their conventional weapons never enabled them to gain.

So if the theories of domestic or foreign aircraft cannot explain the large numbers of almost certainly manufactured UFOs seen for more than a half-century in almost every part of the world, is it possible that these UFOs could be neither domestic nor what is usually considered to be foreign?

Some UFOs May Be Alien

At first glance, the idea that some UFOs may be vehicles from outside the Earth seems utterly preposterous, the baseless result of wishful thinking by highly unscientific minds. If alien craft ever reach our planet, wouldn't they first be detected and identified by scientists, rather than by casual observers? Their nature and origins should be determined by appropriately trained individuals, and the news revealed by high-ranking journalists, not by self-appointed experts with no formal preparation for such a momentous assignment.

As improbable as the presence of non-terrestrial craft in the Earth's vicinity may be, the likelihood of such a presence seems to be increasing by the week, thanks to developments in the new and well-accepted science of astrobiology. Astrobiology is the search for evidence of living things in outer space: complex pre-biotic molecules, large quantities of water, meteorite-borne fossils and Earth-like planets orbiting distant stars.

When authoritative reports of radical-design craft having spectacular performance are viewed in the light of a stream of astrobiological discoveries, the possibility that some UFOs are alien does not seem quite so farfetched. Serious-minded scientists in astronomy and other disciplines estimate there could be billions of planets in the universe, and millions that could harbor life. If even a few of those planets were occupied by technological civilizations, their ability (if not desire) to explore other worlds, such as ours, must be a possibility.

The eventual discovery of, or contact by, one or more alien civilizations is assumed. A search of nearby space for unmanned probes sent by alien civilizations is now being seriously considered, since we have been sending unmanned probes to planets in our solar system for many years. The similarity between these probes and UFOs is hard to ignore.

Hundreds of thousands of UFO sightings have been made by persons in all walks of life, in all parts of the world. Tens of thousands of UFO reports have been made to governmental and private agencies in the past 55-plus years. Thousands of these reports have withstood careful scrutiny and appear to represent real objects having a novel nature.

Patterns of these UFOs' appearance and behavior suggest a limited range of sizes and shapes of unidentified craft, despite the often-desperate efforts on the part of the American and other governments to discount them as nothing more substantial than mistakes made by naive individuals. Their performance, observed repeatedly by expert witnesses, remains as far off the scale today as it was in the 1940s.

If even one of these unidentified UFOs turns out to be an alien craft, the impact on all aspects of our nation's culture—economic, political, personal—will be limited only by what is learned from an open, serious, objective study of the subject.

A DOCTOR RECALLS PHOTOGRAPHING UFOS OVER PHOENIX

Lynne D. Kitei

Lynne D. Kitei is a physician at the Arizona Heart Institute's Imaging/Prevention/Wellness Center in Phoenix. She has been a health reporter and medical consultant for several television stations and has won many awards for the health education videos she has produced. Kitei claims that she had no interest in UFOs until she and her husband began seeing mysterious lights in the night sky from the window of their home in Phoenix. These UFOs were seen by thousands of people on the night of March 13, 1997, but Dr. Kitei had photographed them two years earlier, as well as on many nights in the weeks preceding the mass sighting. She became a key witness to the event and her pictures were shown on television newscasts. In the following selection from her book, *The Phoenix Lights*, she describes what she saw.

The mystery of the Phoenix Lights began for me at 8 P.M. on my birthday eve, February 6, 1995. I had just settled into a bath. The hot water and vanilla-scented bubbles filled my senses with a delicious calm.

Suddenly the mellow moment was shattered by my husband's frantic call, "Come in here quick and look at this. What *is* it?" He sounded alarmed, so I didn't waste any time. Alarm is out of character for Frank, a family physician who has seen it all. I grabbed a towel and, dripping wet, rushed to his side. He was standing transfixed by the bedroom window, looking at something close to the house. From this window I usually scan the twinkling city skyline in the distance, but this time something else caught my attention. Less than a hundred yards away from our property, three objects hung in midair, about 50 to 75 feet above the ground. I immediately looked underneath and around them to see if something or someone was creating the spectacle, but I saw nothing. No laser beam, no hologram. Except for the soft light within each object, there was only darkness. I stood there intently taking it all in. It seemed important not to move.

I took a mental note of every nuance—size, shape, color, distance.

Lynne D. Kitei, *The Phoenix Lights*. Charlottesville, VA: Hampton Roads Publishing, 2004. Copyright © 2000 by Lynne D. Kitei, MD. Reproduced by permission.

Each sphere was an oval, between three and six feet across. They seemed to be hovering motionlessly in perfect symmetry, one on top and the other two aligned underneath, like a pyramid. The soothing amber light contained within each orb looked different from any light I had ever seen. It didn't glare at all and was uniform throughout, reminding me of a holiday luminary that shines from within, without the light extending beyond its edge. Frank and I were in awe, mesmerized by the extraordinary scene.

Photographic Proof

I knew no one else would believe this unless we had photographic proof, so I turned to grab our 35-mm camera from the bedroom closet. "Get back here. Look what's happening now. One of them is disappearing," said Frank. I clutched the camera and hurried to the window. The top oval orb was slowly fading. It was meticulously and uniformly disappearing in place, as though it were being controlled by a dimmer switch.

I wanted to get a shot of this impressive phenomenon, whatever it was. I quickly opened the sliding glass door, stepped out onto the balcony and snapped a picture of the two remaining orbs.

How is this astonishing sight even possible? I wondered, noticing the eerie silence, as if time had stopped. The next thing I remember, the left bottom oval started to dissipate, just like the first, slowly and silently fading from view without moving. I took another photo.

In the days that followed, Frank didn't really want to discuss it. To me, the whole experience was exciting and wondrous. Even so, it didn't make sense, especially when I stared at the place where the three mysterious objects had appeared and then dissolved. For weeks afterward, it felt as though they were still there—watching.

It took me more than two weeks to build up the courage to seek out a film shop. When I finally arrived at the photo lab on February 24, 1995, I timidly admitted to the developer that my husband and I had seen something quite unusual outside our window a couple of weeks before. I asked her to please take special care in trying to find some lights among the photos on the two rolls I handed her.

One of the other developers overheard our conversation. He didn't live far from us, he said, and had seen air force jets scouting our area the day after this sighting. Why would the military be zooming at low altitudes around a private residential area? I added this to a growing list of questions about the mysterious lights.

When the photos came back I discovered that only one picture of the lights had turned out, but what a picture it was. I had caught the lower left oval as it was disappearing while the right oval was still in place. . . .

This single print proved to me that what we had seen was not an optical illusion. But what to do with it? Neither my husband nor I was ever into the topic of Unidentified Flying Objects. We didn't know anyone else who was, either, so I ended up mounting the unique photo on our fireplace mantel, just for fun. It seemed so out of place next to our family pictures that I eventually tucked it neatly behind a favorite portrait for safekeeping. Even though the picture was out of sight, the event wasn't out of my mind.

The Lights Return

Over the next 23 months there wasn't a glimmer of anything unusual in the Phoenix skies. From time to time I wondered what we had seen. If we had been anywhere else in the house, we would probably have missed it. I was relieved that I had captured a photo of the strange incident; otherwise no one, including ourselves, would have believed it had occurred. After something inexplicable happens to you, with no outside confirmation, you begin to doubt the experience and your perception of it, especially over time. As much as I tried to deny it, the feeling that we were supposed to witness and film the mysterious sight lingered. Maybe one day I would find out why.

Then it happened again, but on a grander scale.

It was about 8 P.M. on the evening of January 22, 1997. I had just slipped into bed and was staring out of our picture window at the beautiful skyline. The view was full of lights: stoplights blinking their green, yellow, and red arrays; car lights whizzing down the main thoroughfares; commercial airplanes crisscrossing the skies as they arrived at and departed from Sky Harbor International Airport.

Then something on the western horizon caught my attention. Three huge amber orbs hung there in a stationary row, strangely similar to the three orbs outside our window in 1995. . . .

I watched them alone. After hovering rock-solid for about three or four minutes they each took a turn in fading out. It looked as if each orb was dissipating from the outside in, from right to left, until all three were gone from view.

The First Video

The next evening, while Frank was at the medical board's monthly meeting, something huge and golden-orange glaring motionlessly in the sky once again caught my attention. Realizing that this sight had to be documented, I grabbed my video camera, scurried out to the pool area, and pressed the record button. After filming 17 seconds of footage, the camera clicked off. The battery had gone dead. A few minutes later, the lights faded to black.

"Honey, you won't believe this," I said to Frank when he came home. "Remember I told you about the three lights in a row last night? Well, about a half an hour ago the same lights appeared in front of South Mountain."

As I pointed to the spot where they had appeared, they suddenly reappeared. "That's them! That's them!" I shouted, running into the house and up the long stairway to grab my camera from the closet. Just as I aimed my camera at this puzzling display, six amber spheres blinked on, in an equidistant line, directly above the three that were already there. The distance across was probably more than a mile. There was nothing I could relate it to, except maybe *Star Trek*.

"Oh, my, Frank, what is that? It looks like a Mothership or a *fleet* of ships."

I got several shots off as the bottom three started to disappear, one by one from right to left. I kept clicking away.

During my frenzy to get the photos, I could hear Frank mutter, "It's probably a blimp. Isn't the Phoenix Open in town?"

I tried in earnest to visualize it being a blimp, but to no avail. The lights were shaped like large orange orbs, and they didn't move at all. The notion that these lights were part of a colossal blimp was implausible.

Searching for an Explanation

I called the newspaper to see if anyone else had reported what I was seeing.

"City desk," said the voice in the newsroom of the *Arizona Republic*.

"Could you tell me what the strange lights are that are hovering right now in front of South Mountain? You should get someone out there to capture the sight on film." As my sentence came to an end, so did the light show. They were gone. There was nowhere else to go with the conversation. Reluctantly, I hung up.

The next morning I felt I had to have an explanation. I wanted to believe that there was a rational explication for the incident. First I phoned the *Arizona Republic* asking if anyone had called the night before to report strange lights. Not a one, said the receptionist.

"Can you tell me who I could contact to find out what they might have been?" I asked.

"Maybe it was an experimental military maneuver," she replied quickly. "Sometimes Luke Air Force Base sends out test flights and they don't report them to the public."

The female lieutenant I spoke to next listened patiently and then responded curtly. "I can tell you that they did not come from Luke and they did not come into Luke. We had nothing to do with them."

Pressing further, I asked, "Could you tell me who I should contact to find out what they were?"

"I have no idea."

Frustrated, I asked, "Would you have a number for a UFO organization?"

She stated emphatically, "No. I certainly would not have that information."

"But there must be someone who knows what they were. My husband and I saw the same thing. We even captured some on videotape. I'm sure there must be a logical explanation. I'm only trying to find out what that might be."

"Well, since it was in front of South Mountain, maybe someone at the airport saw something."

"Good idea," I said. I hung up and looked for the Sky Harbor International Airport telephone number.

Another Witness

The strange phenomena had to have come from somewhere. I would just search until I found an answer. Finally, I got the Federal Aviation Administration on the line. I reiterated my account. The operator asked me to hold while she checked to see if the air traffic controllers had seen anything unusual the night before. It was at least five minutes before she returned.

"You're in luck. One of the controllers who is here this morning was working last night. He did see some strange lights. He's not sure what they were."

"Could I speak with him personally?" I requested. She asked me to wait.

Finally, there was a click on the line. A deep male voice asked, "Did you see those six orange lights hovering equidistant from each other in a formation last night about 8:30 P.M.?"

When I told him we had, he seemed almost relieved that someone else had seen them.

"When we saw the array of six lights appear at 8:30 P.M., out of nowhere, we immediately looked on radar, but nothing showed up," he said. "We then thought maybe they were lights carried by skydivers. But that would be unlikely because it was too late and they were in a perfect formation. They couldn't have been flares either. Flares drift downwards. These stayed right in place. Besides, they were a different color from anything I've ever seen. So we grabbed our binoculars to take a closer look. What startled us was that they were six distinct amber objects, hovering motionless for a time, in perfect synchrony."

I was more curious than ever. "So," I inquired again, "what were they?"

There was silence for several seconds, then a deep breath. "Beats me," he answered.

"Wait a minute. You're an air traffic controller. That's what you do, identify things flying around in air space. And you don't know what they were?"

He hesitated for a moment and then replied, "I'll ask around.". . .

Every night that week was filled with curiosity and amazement, viewing these strange amber creations appearing motionless in formations across the horizon. Whatever these lights were, you could see distinctly that the commercial airlines coming in and out of Sky Harbor Airport, about 20 miles from us, were dwarfed by the gigantic orange luminaries.

On January 30, I stepped onto the veranda to capture another silent sighting on video. As the camera rolled, I began my verbal documentation. "This one has been out there for some time."

I put the camera on the balcony ledge so it would be stable and started chatting with Frank, who had joined me. "There were just two there. This one is really high." It was definitely higher than the red lights of the radio tower on South Mountain, which ruled out the possibility that it was someone on the mountain holding a light.

I had taken the 35-mm film of the January 23 sighting to the developer, but to my dismay, none of these photos turned out. I was told that the negatives were blank, and they looked it. Maybe the orbs had been too far away. After all, the ones in the pictures I had taken two years before had been just beyond our house. Now the lights were appearing at a distance. Disappointed, I put the negatives in a drawer. [Later, Dr. Kitei discovered that these negatives did contain images.]

But the recent events were too compelling to dismiss. I started sharing them with my close friends. When they saw the videos, they were dumbfounded. No one could explain the formations. Even though the tapes didn't do them justice, because the orbs appeared much smaller, whiter, and flickered in the videos, the sight of these stationary balls hovering over the mountains was still remarkable.

Still a Mystery

Aside from the verification from the air traffic controller on January 24, there was no other mention of the strange lights, including in the media. I began thinking that, like in 1995, these sightings would remain a mystery.

Whatever they were, I still felt compelled to film them when they reappeared. A little after 9 P.M. on March 4, Frank and I were on the bedroom balcony. He was facing me, leaning against the upstairs railing with the spectrum of white city lights as a backdrop. I forget what we were talking about, but suddenly something amber appeared in the sky right behind Frank's head. "Hold that thought," I blurted, as I rushed into the bedroom to grab the camera.

Frank said he saw something come out of the first one. By the time I got outside, there were two lights very closely aligned, one directly on top of the other. . . .

Frank had given me a telescope for my birthday, which I now focused on the lights. Looking through the eyepiece, I could see that the lights were round, amber-colored balls of swirling energy. No parachutes, no sparks, no smoke trails, no wings in sight. What's more, the spinning orbs didn't move out of frame for the duration of the sighting, about seven minutes.

The next night Frank and I had just entered the bedroom when we noticed through our big window two glowing orbs in the west. They seemed to be hovering directly over the Dial Building downtown. Frank took over the narration, "Wednesday, March 5th, 1997, and this time the light is much farther to the west. It's way over to the west. I would guess about 19th Avenue, perhaps 35th. We just noticed it . . . yep . . . it's gone."

Within seconds, another light appeared in the same spot. When the orbs blinked on, Frank couldn't resist their fascination either. He spoke excitedly. "It's on again. Appears to be one yellow light now."

"What time is it?" I interrupted, then answered myself. "About 8:30, Wednesday evening. And it's orange."

Frank interjected, "Nah. . . . it's yellow."

I compromised. "Orangey-yellow."

"Yellowy-orange," countered Frank, and chanted, "You like tomato . . . I like *tomaato*." The unknown object started fading from view as Frank jokingly whispered, "It's cloaking."

Hope for an Answer

Mid-morning on Thursday, March 6, my son's phone started ringing. I usually don't answer it, but something told me I should.

"Hello," said a strong male voice. "Is Lynne there, please?"

"Speaking," I said.

"Hi, this is Vern at the airport. I was just wondering if you heard anything more about the lights we saw back in January."

"You were going to find out what they were. Did you?"

"I asked around, but nobody here knew what they were. Did you hear anything?"

"I haven't heard a thing, but I've been filming them. Haven't you been seeing them?"

He said "no" and then conjectured that perhaps the lights were behind the ridgeline of South Mountain, obstructing them from the view of anyone lower than we were, which included the airport. That would mean that each light was enormous, much bigger than a commercial aircraft.

Still no answers, only more questions. The newspaper and Luke Air Force Base had snubbed me, so where else could I turn?

After searching out someone associated with a credible UFO organization, I was finally referred to Richard, a field investigator for MUFON, the Mutual UFO Network. After I briefly described the picture I had taken of the February 1995 sighting and the appearance of the recent lights, we set up an appointment to meet at his home offfice on March 12. He asked if the current state director of MUFON, Tom Taylor, could attend. It was curious that neither of the men had heard about the strange lights, but they were eager to analyze my photos. At the least, I hoped they could tell me what I had been filming.

The huge amber orbs continued their nightly visits, usually three sightings in succession with several minutes in between, reappearing in just about the same place. On March 10, things got more cryptic. While I was downstairs cleaning up after dinner, I heard Frank call out, urging me to come upstairs. When I got there, he said that I had just missed an astounding formation of three orbs intersecting four orbs. It was amusing to see him so excited about the lights, particularly since he usually teased me during the mysterious nightly visitations. He drew a sketch of the formation, so I could visualize it. Sadly, we didn't capture it on film.

Meanwhile, I was bursting with curiosity, counting the hours until my meeting with the UFO investigator. But that meeting was not to take place, at least not on the day we had planned. [March 14, the morning after the lights were witnessed by thousands of citizens, was coincidentally the date of Dr. Kitei's rescheduled appointment with the investigator. Her video of the lights appeared on all Phoenix TV channels' evening newscasts.]

ALIEN ABDUCTIONS ARE REAL

Budd Hopkins and Carol Rainey

Budd Hopkins is a prominent UFO abduction investigator who has written several books about the cases he has studied. Carol Rainey is his wife. The following selection, which summarizes their view of the abduction phenomenon, comes from the opening and closing pages of their book Sight Unseen: Science, UFO Invisibility and Transgenic Beings. *Hopkins and Rainey believe that the aliens are taking reproductive material from the people they abduct and are producing hybrid children by means of genetic engineering. Under hypnosis, a great many individuals have uncovered memories of this process, although most researchers— even among those convinced that aliens are on Earth—feel that there may be other explanations for such memories. Unlike some people with memories of UFO encounters who prefer to be called "experiencers" rather than "abductees," the ones Budd Hopkins has studied perceive the aliens as unfriendly and view them as a threat to humankind.*

In the year 2001, I [Budd Hopkins,] marked a quarter-century of investigation into the UFO abduction phenomenon. When I first began to examine accounts of alien abduction in 1976, researchers were aware of only a handful of these bizarre and intriguing reports. Although the incidents were apparently unrelated, they were often described by highly credible witnesses. As the years passed I received thousands of reports and was able to closely investigate hundreds that revealed striking similarities. Unrelated individuals each described similar specific details, further adding to the credibility of the witnesses, and as I examined and compared these cases, I was able to detect many recurring patterns. Portentous in the extreme, these patterns seemed to point inexorably to one plausible interpretation: Intelligent, nonhuman beings possessing a technology vastly superior to our own have arrived on our planet.

Even more disturbing, these enigmatic visitors have apparently embarked upon a covert, highly systematic program in which thousands

Budd Hopkins and Carol Rainey, *Sight Unseen: Science, UFO Invisibility and Transgenic Beings.* New York: Pocket Books, 2004. Copyright © 2003 by Budd Hopkins and Carol Rainey. Reproduced with permission of Atria Books, an imprint of Simon & Schuster Adult Publishing Group.

of our men, women, and children are repeatedly lifted out of their everyday lives. They are removed from their cars, backyards, beds, and schools and subjected to a methodical regimen of examination, study, and sample-taking. Though UFO investigators have amassed a great deal of information about the UFO occupants' methods and the nature of their interest in us, we are still uncertain as to their ultimate plans, for our planet and for the human race. Various scenarios have been proposed; few offer much peace of mind.

It has taken years of careful comparative research to isolate scores of highly specific recurring patterns within what had at first seemed an idiosyncratic, almost random collection of incidents. At the present time we can confidently define the abduction phenomenon as a distinct body of hard-edged, precisely detailed, mutually corroborative recurring events that have involved thousands of individuals from all over the world.

Scars and Screen Memories

As I looked into case after case one common pattern that I discovered has to do with particular types of scars found on individuals after abduction experiences, apparently the result of quasimedical sample-taking procedures carried out by the UFO occupants. These telltale lesions are of two main types: circular, "scoop marks"—depressions one to two centimeters in diameter and several millimeters deep—and neat, straightline, "surgical" cuts ranging from two to nine centimeters in length. I have seen perhaps one hundred scoop marks—the more common of the two types and often appearing on the lower leg—and scores of straight-line cuts. Several physicians have noticed the similarity of scoop marks to the scars left by punch biopsies, but X rays and other forms of medical examination have not yet led to a consistent theory as to why these marks were made.

The "screen memory" phenomenon is another pattern that I uncovered shortly after I began my investigations. A "screen memory" results when UFO occupants somehow substitute more palatable conventional imagery for an abductee's traumatic recollections. Instead of recalling unnerving alien faces with large, impenetrable black eyes and gray, hairless skin, abductees have frequently reported conscious, prehypnotic memories of such things as five-foot-tall wingless owls; gray, hairless, upright cats; or deer with expressive black eyes that communicate mind-to-mind. In one case, what was first perceived as a pileup of six wrecked automobiles with their headlights ablaze eventually revealed itself as a landed UFO, and in another case, a huge, motionless silver airplane initially stood in for a UFO in the sunny sky. The idea that these images are not self-generated but are implanted in the minds of abductees by their captors is supported by the fact that two or more people in the same encounter saw exactly the same (impossible) five-foot-tall owl staring at them, the same pileup of six empty cars on a deserted road, or the same telepathic deer.

Scoop marks, straight-line scars, and screen memories are just a few of the many recurring patterns that have been documented by researchers in literally thousands of abduction cases throughout the world. Among the more than five hundred abductees I have personally worked with over the past quarter century, there are African-Americans, Catholics, musicians, a NASA research scientist, Mormons, medical doctors, Japanese, Muslims, Scotsmen, farmers, Israelis, nurses, Orthodox Jews, Brazilians, Protestant ministers, Australians, scientists, Hispanics, policemen, Hindus, actors, Canadians, psychiatrists, airline pilots, military officers, businesspeople, engineers, artists, students, professors—and even a prostitute or two. Their encounters with nonhuman occupants of UFOs have taken place in the city and the country, in forests and front yards, in groups or individually. These encounters are neither imaginary nor "imaginal"—whatever that portmanteau word actually means. They are not the results of hallucinations, sleep paralysis, or hoaxes. The skilled UFO researcher has learned how to identify such mundane explanations, thus avoiding pursuit of any vague, dubious, and unsupported accounts.

A Truly Extraordinary Phenomenon

Out of the mass of credible reports that remain, the supporting physical, medical, and photographic evidence is so consistent that *none* of the debunkers' psychological or psychosocial theories can begin to explain it away. Over the years, for better or for worse, I have come to believe that UFO abductions are real, event-level occurrences. They constitute a truly extraordinary phenomenon, and it would seem a truism that an extraordinary phenomenon *demands* an extraordinary investigation.

This brings us to one of the truly great human mysteries: that five decades of these consistent and alarming findings have escaped the attention of mainstream science. Not one penny of the National Science Foundation's budget or the National Institutes of Health's (NIH) $20.3 billion research budget has ever been applied to investigation of the UFO abduction phenomenon. . . . Not one academic institution takes the phenomenon seriously enough to develop an accredited program of study around it. There have been, certainly, a few courageous individual scientists and scholars who have hacked paths into the tangled UFO jungle of skeptical hyperbole, myth, ridicule, and misidentification and found their way into the broad clearing of credible eyewitness reports. Unfortunately, many of those who have publicly announced themselves as being seriously interested in investigating the UFO mystery have paid dearly for their courage with professional careers that have been blighted by intolerant, even outraged colleagues.

Researcher Richard Hall has said that we have two possibilities of obtaining meaningful answers to the UFO dilemma: one; if science and government wake up and begin to support its thorough investigation; and two; if the aliens decide to communicate their intent to us and make their presence undeniable. But, unfortunately, none of the parties involved seem very partial to either of these possibilities.

One would think that the implications of the UFO mystery—which include the possible end of human culture and existence as we know it—would evoke a terrible outcry, a groundswell of demands to look into these reports. But this is not happening, especially at the governmental and scientific levels, where scorn and disavowal of interest in the subject prevail. We believe this is due less to concern about the potential danger of covert extraterrestrial presence than to the widespread tenet in the realms of government, science, and the media that it is just not possible.

As for the aliens, rather than the proverbial broadcast from the White House lawn, the aliens seem quite content with their program of secrecy. And why not? Whatever their ultimate purpose, they are able to dip in and out of our world with impunity. They don't have to tell us what they are doing, because—to the best of our knowledge—no government, no power on earth is holding them accountable. . . .

The Authors' Differing Views

The actual range of . . . firsthand testimony [about the aliens' behavior] is far more consistent than the bewildering range of opinions theorists have issued about the meaning of it all. On one end of the scale is what we might call the ultraparanoid interpretation: that the aliens are demons, beings who have come here to capture and devour our children, to use human body parts as replacements, and to feast upon what General Buck Turgison in [the movie] *Dr. Strangelove* called our "vital bodily fluids." There is not, in our opinion, a scintilla of evidence supporting such a dire and melodramatic reading of the data.

On the other end of the spectrum is the idea—*hope* is perhaps a better word—that the aliens are here as quasi-god-like beings to help us with our problems, to heal our damaged planet, and to offer what has been called, with a straight face, "unconditional love." No one who reads the accounts we have been presenting can come to such a rosy—and simplistic—conclusion. The truth is, of course, that we do not know the future. We do not know the aliens' ultimate intentions, nor do we really know what their options are. . . .

[We,] Hopkins and Rainey, have somewhat differing views about alien intent. We do not share the same balance between hope and pessimism.

Carol Rainey's Opinion

On the one hand, Rainey suggests:

> What the ETs may be creating are not hybrids at all but transgenic human beings. It is both biologically possible and would

best fit the profile of a secretive, invasive force that might be intent on conquering us from within—or equally possible, healing or altering the genes that no longer work for us in our present environment. The change could happen one genetic code word at a time—or an entire chromosome at a time. Either way, if the genes to be modified were carefully and expertly selected over thousands of years, we might never notice what was happening. The Hollywood-style massive destruction and cultural devastation seen in the movie *Independence Day* would never have to be played out. Biologists tell us that an entire species can do most of its changing internally, with new species traits only gradually manifesting themselves in outward appearance and behavior. If this is indeed occurring, will these alterations be good for the humans—or bad for the humans?

This is a difficult issue to take in both emotionally and intellectually: The subtle but inexorable alteration of the human species. But it may very well be that a culture several million years in advance of our own has already mastered the technology of bioengineering. The basic building blocks of life—proteins, amino acids, sugars, etc.—appear to be the same throughout the universe. The question is: How different are the issues and problems of altering the lifeforms on Earth from those of other planets—or even, perhaps, in other dimensions? On Earth, as most biologists will tell you, the process is complex, intertwined with other systems, and not yet well enough understood to be predictable and safe for human use. With no federal or institutional support at all, and with only a handful of mainstream scientists willing or able to risk ridicule and loss of funding, people worldwide who are experiencing the UFO abduction phenomenon firsthand have little choice. They can only hope and pray that these alien beings know what they're doing.

Budd Hopkins's Opinion

On the other hand, Hopkins cautions, in such a transaction the odds favor us losing and the aliens gaining. He states:

The twenty-seven years I have spent working with abductees, listening to their traumatic encounters, and trying to help them heal a lifetime of psychic damage, have left me hardened to reassuring talk of "beings of light" practicing benevolent "tough love." I have seen too much pain to allow myself more than a life-sustaining modicum of hope. And yet, I may be wrong. Though abductions inevitably leave the abductees scarred, emotionally and psychologically, there is no sign that this kind of psychic damage was intended. In fact, there are many indications that the UFO occupants try to minimize the pain and emotional damage their activities naturally inflict. *Amoral* is a useful word in this content, less brutal than other terms I could use with equal justice.

And yet . . . the future is still the uncertain future, and the alien mind is still mysteriously alien. We do not know their real attitude toward our own humanity as it is now, with most of Earth's population as yet untouched by forced genetic manipulation. We do not know how the aliens view our inherent qualities of spirituality, physical diversity, romantic love, humor and sexuality. Or our intensely protective love for our children, our rich artistic expressiveness, and our willingness to sacrifice our own selves for the greater good. How many of these basic human qualities—attributes in which the aliens seem to sadly deficient—do they truly envy and wish to append to their own narrow natures? Might they be willing to complete their program of genetic manipulation, successfully merging their ominous "paranormal" abilities with our frail but splendid human characteristics, and then leave to populate another place, to seed another developing race of intelligent beings?

What *are* their ultimate intentions? Are we merely a race of modern Aztecs hoping that the Spaniards will either get back in their boats and sail away or turn out to be benevolent gods? Do we, like the ancient Mexicans, need to turn a blind eye to the third possibility: that our alien visitors will instead turn out to be the ultimate conquistadors? For myself, I carefully nurture the seed of a fragile optimism. Admittedly it's a tiny seed, threatened on every side by inhospitable conditions, but I feed and water that tiny seed every day, and quietly hope it grows.

CROSS-BREEDING HUMANS WITH ALIENS IS NOT IMPOSSIBLE

William R. Alschuler

William R. Alschuler is a professor of science at California Institute of the Arts and has also taught at University of California, Santa Cruz; Harvard; and MIT. He is the author or editor of four books dealing with the astronomical search for extraterrestrial intelligence (SETI) or with UFOs. Alschuler does not think it is likely that extraterrestrials have come to Earth, but he is open to the idea that they could do so. The following selection comes from *The Science of UFOs*, in which he offers explanations for the observed behavior of UFOs and extraterrestrials that are consistent with today's knowledge of science. Although he does not believe that extraterrestrials are actually producing human/alien hybrids, here he explains why he doesn't consider such cross-breeding impossible in principle. He also explains why genetic evidence shows it's improbable that humans are descended from aliens.

I am now going to take a position that may surprise some readers. Because I believe that amino acids identical to ours are widespread in the galaxy, and because it is likely that only our type of DNA can manipulate them, I think aliens and alien life in general will turn out to be biochemically like us. Therefore those abductees who claim that aliens are running a cross-breeding that mixes us and them cannot be proved wrong *in principle*. In principle, I think such a thing would be possible.

It used to be thought that interspecies exchange of genetic material was impossible. But evidence in nature has been found that bacteria have transported some genes and gene fragments from one species to another. Our DNA contains code that is also found in some viruses. The latter is evidence that viruses were our ancestors or that, more likely, they infected our ancestors. Our cells contain structures called mitochondria—their energy factories—that billions of years ago were almost certainly independent bacteria that took up a symbiotic relationship with other, larger cells, and stayed on. Mitochondria contain

DNA independent of nuclear DNA, which descends only from the mother. So our body chemistry has "alien" bits in it of a sort.

Would such a cross-breeding program be simple? No. It would be immensely difficult. Recently, we have genetically engineered the genes for the human immune system into mice. This cutting edge technique allows us to test immune related drugs in mice and expect to get a response reliably predictive of the human response. This, however, is mere child's play compared to a human/alien crossbreed. The latter would be equivalent in difficulty to trying to cross humans with terrestrial species outside our immediate families. It would be at least as difficult as crossing humans with seals or dogs, and more likely as difficult as crossing us with reptiles, fish, or birds—or even with some of the complex creatures that don't fit in any known phylum that went extinct shortly after appearing on the terrestrial scene 550 million years ago. . . .

Genetic Engineering Would Be Difficult

First, no ordinary cross-breeding by mating or grafting would work. Normal fertilization would fail; the graft would not take. Embryo jumbling would almost certainly fail due to the genetic distance between species. The one case we have where embryo-bashing succeeded was that of the "geep," carried out at the University of California at Davis in 1987. The embryonic cells of a sheep and goat were combined and implanted in a ewe, where they grew into a fetus, which was born and raised to adulthood. The geep was female, with the head and neck of a goat and the body of a sheep, and was later able to carry an implanted sheep embryo to term. But it was sterile. And this example represents a combination of *very* closely related species.

The only techniques with a chance of success are the new techniques of genetic engineering. Here the knowledge we are missing includes, but is not limited to:

1. How changes to DNA affect the form of the species. Recent discoveries about the HOX gene have begun to reveal the secrets of developmental changes and the placement and numbers of limbs and organs.
2. How DNA controls metabolism, in detail.
3. How DNA structure affects the biochemistry of reproduction.
4. How the DNA controls the structure and operations of the immune system.

This last item is a matter of intense interest to us already as it is key to understanding cell and organ transplant rejection. The normal human immune system recognizes from the fetal stage more than a million different substances that it can defend against. Until the late 1800s so little was known about this that people died when transfused with the wrong blood type. The very existence of immunologically different blood types was not then known. Transplants from other humans, with only a few exceptions, and cross-species transplants, are eventually rejected with a usually fatal reaction. We give transplant patients immune suppressing drugs to prevent that, but all these drugs knock down the whole system, leaving the patient open to just about any infection.

The distance from our current state of knowledge in this area to the state that would permit interspecies cross breeding is *immense*. But I don't know of any physical or biological law that such a manipulation would violate. And any aliens have likely been around a lot longer than we have. Having taken the leap that it is in principle possible, do I think that such a program is now underway? I don't think so, but for reasons unrelated to the problems of genetics itself. Even if we are currently being visited by aliens, the logic of their carrying on such a program—with the apparent uncertainty and the crude surgical techniques reported by abductees—completely escapes me. The objection that "aliens are aliens" in thought and deed and thus unknowable is not viable. Surely any starfaring species has command of all the genetic knowledge it needs to do exactly what we have described above, and will have done any cross-breeding either with species native to their home planet or will have the knowledge to construct new species (like us) from scratch by molecular assembly of DNA or their analog of it. Their techniques would likely never involve any substantial sampling by penetration, much less failures to correctly anesthetize the subject during such a procedure.

Could We Be Descendants of Aliens?

Science fiction and some abductee accounts suggest that we are really descendants of alien species. In some cases our ancestors allegedly landed here 10,000 to 100,000 years ago. In others, we are said to have evolved from alien trash. Neither of these scenarios is likely, based on examination of the evidence, both genetic and geological.

The genetic evidence was mentioned above: by sampling contemporary species we can trace genetic consanguinity and easily show that all terrestrial life shares some parts of its DNA, and we can estimate how long ago each species had an ancestor in common with each other species. Then, with radiological absolute dating techniques, we can show that the ancestors of living species seem to fit this picture at least in some cases. In the case of amber-preserved insects we can get both a geologic age and, from extracted DNA (*à la* [novelist Michael] Crichton's *Jurassic Park*), a molecular DNA age.

While it is true that the fossil record of early humans is relatively poorly known, it is well enough sampled to show a reasonably clear line of descent back into the pre-primates of about 6 million years ago. And it is reasonable to expect that the picture will eventually become more or less complete. The million-plus-year-old footprints of adult and child preserved together in volcanic ash in Africa clearly demonstrate that fundamental human family values go way back. There is just no room for alien interlopers.

Given the evidence of 2.8-billion-year-old strands of algae cells from the Gunflint formation and the stromatolite fossils (compacted algal colonies) found around the world that date back to 3.8 billion years ago or older, which both look essentially identical to contemporary examples, it is hard to believe that life began other than as the result of the rain of cosmic amino acids and other chemicals onto Earth after it cooled down following its formation 4.5 billion years ago. It is the simplest explanation.

Panspermia and Interstellar Epidemics

At the turn of the twentieth century the Swedish chemist Svante Arrhenius put forth the theory of panspermia. It is roughly similar to the idea of the cosmic catapult tree from [science fiction author James] Blish's *A Case of Conscience*. Arrhenius suggested that life might evolve forms so hardy that they could survive the voyage between the stars, and that over time life would spread from planet to planet and star system to star system. This now seems relatively unlikely though not absolutely ruled out. The detection of amino acids in meteorites makes it likely that what spreads are the building blocks of life.

The conditions of space seem too hostile to allow true life to evolve. Each level of complexity involves more interactions for success, and the low densities of matter even in dense interstellar clouds, along with the deep chill there, make such interactions improbable.

This did not stop [astronomer] Sir Fred Hoyle and his colleagues from suggesting back in the 1970s that some of the viruses and bacteria that infect our world have evolved in outer space and that they have rained down on us in cometary debris as it falls to Earth. To some extent such space junk falls all the time. But the notion that bacteria and viruses can evolve on comets seems unlikely on the grounds outlined above, though it should be noted that comets are composed partly of water ice. But that ice probably sublimes directly to gas as the comet is heated up as it approaches the Sun, bypassing the liquid state.

Could alien incoming viruses and bacteria infect us? Since I have argued that they would likely be made of the same amino acids and similar DNA, it is not ruled out. But the probability of infecting us, having lived for eons in a frozen state, seems unlikely. Think of all the viruses and bacteria already here that do *not* infect us.

An Abductee Recalls Six Hours Spent Aboard a UFO

Jack, as told to Preston Dennett

Preston Dennett is a field investigator for the Mutual UFO Network (MUFON) who is the author of several books. The following selection is an account of a UFO experience reported to him by a man he calls "Jack." (Most UFO abductees do not seek publicity and do not allow their real names to be published.) Dennett and others maintain that comparatively few people who remember contact with UFOs can do so consciously; in most cases, these memories emerge only while they are under hypnosis. Sometimes, however, a "trigger mechanism" causes a person to recall a UFO event that took place days, or even years, earlier. For Jack, the trigger was the intense pain of a cracked tooth, which suddenly brought to mind what had happened to him twenty-five years before when he was twelve years old. He had gone with his mother and younger brother to a drive-in movie, and on the way home it was very foggy. When they were almost there the car stopped. His mother and brother saw a strange animal in the road that looked like a spotted skunk three feet tall, though Jack didn't. Then the whole car lit up and something bright appeared overhead; his mother thought it was a crop duster, but he knew it couldn't be. It suddenly "winked out" and the car started—but when they got home the sun was coming up and it was six o'clock in the morning, not midnight. They had lost six hours. As Dennett explains, Jack became aware of other strange facts in the years that followed, but not until he cracked his tooth did he remember what occurred during the missing time.

It began with the 1972 sighting of what appeared to be a giant spotted skunk traipsing down the road in the middle of a foggy summer night. As soon as they saw the strange creature, Jack's mother and brother began exclaiming wildly. Jack, however, couldn't see any-

Preston Dennett, *Extraterrestrial Visitations*. St. Paul, MN: Llewellyn Publications, 2001. Copyright © 2001 by Preston Dennett. Reproduced by permission.

thing. It was then that a bright white light struck the car and Jack remembers feeling a floating, weightless sensation. His next conscious memory at the time was the car starting up and then heading home.

But the cracked tooth brought to the surface what really happened. The light hit the car and then Jack felt himself being pulled out of the car and up into the air. As Jack clearly remembered, "The next thing I know, I just kind of felt weightless . . . I remember the car kind of floating, too, a little bit. The car was floating, like, side-to-side while my mom was still seeing this thing out the window. She stopped and the car was kind of floating, not really floating, but almost floating. And then when we stopped completely, it came straight up the road at us, and it was like two bright lights. Then they kind of came together, pointed right at us, and that's when I floated up out of the car. And I kind of floated out the side window of the car, which was rolled down. The next thing I remember is just kind of being upside down and thinking, 'Hey, this is pretty cool. I'm kind of, like, weightless.' And seeing my mom and my brother with just like a frozen expression, like nothing. I'm floating upside down. My mom, I could see her trying to move. And as I'm going up, I thought, 'Man, I'm going up! Wow! I'm going up into this thing! There's nothing I can do about it. I'm going.'"

Taken Aboard

As he rose up into the craft, Jack's greatest concern was for his family. "I remember saying, literally telling them when I was floating up there, 'Hey, I don't want you to take my mom or my brother or do anything.' And they said, 'Don't worry, we're not going to hurt you.' Well, not really said, but this was the impression that I got. 'We're not going to hurt them. Don't worry about them.' I remember looking down at my brother, and I'm kind of floating in mid-air. And he's just got this little stupid-looking grin on his face, just frozen. It was really strange."

Jack couldn't see what was lifting him into the air. Not only was it too bright to comfortably look at, but he was hanging upside down and was understandably disoriented. His next memory is of being taken inside the craft and floated onto a table. "The next thing I remember is kind of getting there, and one of them kind of knew me. I don't know if you would say 'knew me,' but knew about me. There was like maybe ten—I can't really call them people or anything, because they were like . . . entities. They were, like, individuals, but yet they weren't. And I don't know what they looked like. This is something that I've really been trying to remember and I cannot remember. I don't know if they were short, tall, big—anything. I just knew that they were there.

"As I moved around in the thing, I was realizing, 'Hey, this thing is big! This is really a big thing I'm on here.' And I remember getting on this one table. And I don't know how to describe it—it kind of like formed to your back. I kind of sunk down into it, but not really. And I remember getting kind of scared. I remember being on this table thing. Then, I remember two of them going back and forth, and it was, like, a 'good cop, bad cop' thing. One of them, for all he cared, just threw me off. That's kind of what the impression was, just like 'get him off here.' And the other one, he wasn't in charge . . . it's so hard to describe something that you have no idea what it was. In the meantime, the other one was saying kind of like, 'No, we are not going to do that' . . . this is what was going on. There was one of them that was like good, but he wasn't the boss. And the one that was the boss was kind of bad, but yet he still listened. I think they were going to really actually do something to me, but this other one kept saying that."

As Jack lay there on the table, the beings began to perform what appeared to be some sort of medical procedure upon him. "I remember them putting something in the bottom of both my feet. . . . I don't know what it was, some kind of thing—a tool-type thing, something in the bottom of both feet . . . I remember cold on my feet. I could remember something physically touching my foot, like a flesh-type thing, but not quite. It's almost like something was holding onto my foot, and then I remember being cold.

"And I remember them telling me to open my mouth, and that's it. Other than that, when it comes to the mouth part, I can't think . . . on that table thing, I do remember them being around me. But then they were kind of indifferent, like they just kind of watched, like a kid with a puzzle being done a hundred times, kind of like, 'yeah,' and a couple of them taking off, like they could care less about what was going on."

Inside the UFO

Although Jack was disoriented and shocked by what was happening to him, he still had the presence of mind to observe his surroundings. His first impression was the sheer size of the craft, which was easily as large as a small building. Everything about the inside of the craft, however, looked strange and unfamiliar. Even today, he finds it difficult to describe. "[It was] kind of beige. It was kind of all the same, like a beige, goldish, bronze color. Bronze, yeah, I guess it would be a bronze color, not shiny though. Like a dull bronze. I don't remember any sharp corners. It was smooth. Everything was kind of smooth . . . no sharp corners . . . [There were] no lights. I mean everything was light, but it was like—how would you describe it? Maybe like those hidden lights, like if you're in a room, you can still read but you know what I'm talking about, those hidden lights? There were no lights exactly . . . I remember when I was in the table-type room thing, it was just kind of like one side of it was open, but yet dimmer. I guess you really wouldn't call it glass. Almost like looking through a piece of plastic . . . it was kind of dim, but when I looked at outside lights, they weren't bright at all."

As far as the temperature of the craft, Jack said, "It wasn't hot, I know that. It wasn't hot or cold. It was just about right." Although Jack remembers looking at the beings, for some reason, he is utterly unable to visualize what they looked like. "Just for the whole life of me, I cannot remember what anything looked like there, any of whatever they were. They were there, but for the life of me, I cannot remember. I even remember thinking, I'm going to look at them now. And I remember turning my head up and looking at them. But I don't remember what was there. You know, I'm almost convinced that these things were ugly, that's why I don't want to remember them. I'm serious, that's what I'm thinking. I think these things were ugly, like scary-looking damn things. I remember not being intimidated by them because I remember looking at eye-level, or almost looking down on them. But then again, I was sitting on that table thing, so it's hard to say. Looking over at them from the table, I was trying to look for a way to get out of there. And there wasn't really like a door or anything. But there was almost like an escalator, but not an escalator. And it went up.

At one point, Jack asked again about his mom and brother back in the car. The answer they gave him was not very comforting. "The reason it was a bad experience for me was because I was scared for my mom and my brother. I wasn't really scared for myself at all. I was worried that they were going to do something to them. And I remember asking them, the good one, what . . . and he said, 'Don't worry about it, we don't want them.' It was like that. 'Don't want them. Don't need them. Don't care.' It was just like, 'We don't care about them. They can just stay there and they'll be fine and you'll be back.'"

Emotionless Beings

As the experience progressed, Jack came to realize that the beings were almost devoid of emotion. Their thought processes were also very different from our own. "It was kind of like these things were like—I don't know—it's kind of like they were indifferent about everything. They had opinions, but I guess you'd kind of say they couldn't make their minds up, like what they were going to do next. I don't know how to explain this part of it. They were really indecisive, almost like they had to take a vote on everything before they did it. I guess that would be a good way to put it. Somebody would come up with an idea, then they would all have to kind of decide about it before they did it. That includes, like, even when I'm on my way up."

What impressed Jack the most about the beings was not so much their indecisiveness but their lack of feelings. "They're indifferent . . . almost machine-like, I'd guess you'd say. It was like no emotions. That's mostly what I would say, like no emotions. Like they could care less. Like just throw me out of the thing and it would have made no difference to him, that one. But the other one was saying, 'No, we can't do that.' But like I said, it was just like a jury on every single thing that the things did. Almost like whatever these things were had a card that said 'yes' on one side and 'no' on another side. Every little thing that was going to happen, they stuck their card up and the majority ruled."

After a while, Jack was floated up off the table and into another part of the craft. He was shocked to find that he never actually walked around, but was floated from room-to-room. "I don't really remember standing. I do kind of remember kneeling, floating, but I don't remember actually physically walking around in this thing. I was just, like, from one place to another."

The View from Above

What would happen next is unique in UFO literature. It would also be Jack's single most vivid and enjoyable part of his experience. Jack suddenly felt the craft move very quickly to another location. He could literally feel the motion of the craft. "I remember kind of shooting in this thing. I'm thinking, 'Boy, this feels really weird.' We kind of like went straight up above the fog. I could look out. The next thing, I was down in this thing. It was like a little clear diamond-thing on the bottom of it [the craft]. I'm in this thing and there are like bungee cords on me . . . I sat in this clear diamond-shape—actually suspended, it almost felt like bungee cords, but I could see everything around. I got, like, a 360-degree view. I could look everywhere. We drop back down and we're by my farm. We're literally down in the pasture above this ditch. And there are some big high voltage power lines, heavy-duty power lines through there. You can just feel the electricity coming off.

"Well as we dropped down to this thing, whatever the clear thing I was in, in the bottom, kind of got smaller. It was kind of like more of a confined space. It seemed wide open to me before, and yet I was enclosed, kind of like plastic or glass."

Jack was totally in awe. It was as if he were dangling outside the bottom of the craft, with a perfect view of everything for miles around. He saw his home below him and all the fields around. The room he was in seemed to be designed specifically for observation. In fact, the whole room would swivel to the direction that he looked. "In places it didn't move at all, like if I just wanted to look one way, it just stayed there. But if I turned, it would . . . move all over. But if I just stopped and looked one way, it would just stop and look one way. And I still remember the country. I was never up in a balloon or a plane or anything over our farm, but I remember exactly the way it looked from the air, exactly, looking down . . . I could see everything around the whole area of my farm. I could see for, like, two miles around."

Sucking Up Electricity

"So anyway, as we went up there, the one . . . who was like the 'good cop guy' kind of starts telling me or showing me—it was like he was explaining to me what they were doing. And I don't know what it was. But we went up to the power lines and after we got back down and that little thing I was in seemed to kind of, like, shrink up inside, four rotating . . . things on each side of this thing—the diamond or triangle or whatever it was—there were four lights that started spinning around. And I could see them from where I was. But then I was back up inside. For some reason, I wasn't down in that thing anymore. I went inside into this room again, but yet we could see out and see what was going on. And I saw those beams suck all together, come into one big beam and hit the power pole, sucking the electricity out of it . . . and these were like, I mean, *lights!* They all focused into one and they started sucking electricity out of the power poles. I can't describe it but I could literally feel it going through my body.

"I remember being cold. That's when they went and sucked up that electricity. That is the most vivid part of the whole thing. And I remember we were up above it, a telephone-pole, maybe two telephone-pole lengths above it. And all those lights focusing into one super bright light—just *pshew!* Just literally seeing the electricity coming out of there, and feeling it. It was just like it drained everything, just took it all.

"Another thing, when I was up in that thing, we were above the fog, just kind of floating right above this fog. And when they went to go suck the electricity out of the power lines, that fog just got out of the way. It just opened wide up—just *shew!*—got out of the way, and I could see crystal clear.

"Another thing, I remember my teeth kind of hurting when it was sucking that stuff up. Just like when you're chewing on aluminum foil. I remember feeling like, 'Hurry up, get this thing over with.' I wanted to go back down into that thing where I was like bungeeing around . . . the one guy, the good cop guy, he was telling me all kinds of stuff, but it wasn't sinking in. I didn't understand what he was telling me. There were math formula things and something about a lot of triangles and circles. There was a lot of geometry thrown at me. And I'm just sitting there thinking, 'This is pretty cool, but I kind of want to go home.' Like, 'Get this done.' . . . The one that was the good one, was trying to tell me this stuff, and the one that was the bad one was not really allowing him to. There was a bunch of whatever they were in the thing, but there was only two that were actually—I guess you could say communicating or whatever.

After this episode, Jack remembers the craft moving very quickly to yet another location. "I remember just shooting off. And the next thing I know is we're, like, somewhere where I don't even know where we are . . . we kind of shot around—like went for a little drive I guess you'd say—shot around. I can still remember the exact direction we took out there. The next thing, we were somewhere where I had no idea."

At this point, Jack's memory remains extremely hazy. Something else may have occurred, but he has no idea what it was, or how long they stayed there. All he really remembers is that the terrain looked totally unfamiliar. After an undetermined amount of time, they left.

Floating to the Car

Jack was somewhat relieved to see that they were back above his car. "And then we were back above the car, no fog. And I remember floating back into the car just floating back over the car, right back where it was, floating upside down. I remember kind of playing around too, flipping, doing flips and kind of thinking it was cool going upside down. I remember getting to the car and kind of looking back up at the thing, and as I'm looking up at it, it's getting smaller and smaller. And I remember saying, 'You didn't do anything to my mom or brother, right?' 'Right, don't worry.' I don't remember floating back in the window, but I remember floating back to the car, seeing my brother, worrying about him breathing . . . I remember floating down, upside down, back into the car into the back seat.

"Then my brother just turned around and said, 'See, I told you that was a crop duster.' . . . Then the car started and we drove about a hundred yards and we pulled into the driveway."

[Editor's note: Twenty-five years later, when the pain of the cracked tooth brought these memories back into Jack's mind, he asked his mother whether she remembered the night when they had gone to the movies and found when they got home that it was six o'clock in the morning instead of midnight. She said that she had been wondering about it all those years, and that she had also been wondering about the strange animal—the three-foot-high skunk—she had seen in the fog, the one Jack didn't see. His brother remembered the animal, too. So there was independent confirmation that something unusual had occurred.]

PSYCHOLOGISTS HAVE CONFLICTING VIEWS OF THE ALIEN ABDUCTION PHENOMENON

Kaja Perina

Kaja Perina is editor in chief of *Psychology Today*. In the following selection she discusses several contrasting views of the alien abduction phenomenon, especially the observations of John Mack, a psychiatrist at Harvard University, and those of psychologists who contested his opinions. As Perina attests, psychological tests show that most people who believe they've come into contact with aliens are neither mentally ill nor faking, but an explanation for their memories that fits all cases is still being sought. Some psychologists believe sleep paralysis is the answer, but that can't apply to those whose experiences occurred while they were wide awake in the daytime. Dr. Mack was the first professional in his field to publicly state that he believed some of his patients had actually been abducted by aliens. His investigation of the issue, however, was cut short when he was killed by a drunk driver in the fall of 2004.

People who believe they've been abducted by aliens have always resided at the farthest fringes of science, and the recent claim by a UFO cult known as the Raelians that they had cloned a human being does little to endear abductees to the mainstream. The sect's leader, Rael, maintains that he was plucked from a volcano by almond-eyed aliens who granted him an audience with Jesus, Buddha and Muhammad, each of whom confirmed that humans are descended from extraterrestrials.

But for every Rael, there are hundreds of workaday individuals who claim to have been abducted by aliens. These individuals do not flower into gurus; they struggle alone with memories of unintelligible messages, temporary paralysis and humanoid creatures hovering over their beds. Their stories don't always check out, but their minds do: Psychological tests confirm that abductees are rarely psychotic or mentally ill. Some 3 million Americans believe they've encountered bright lights and incurred strange bodily marks indicative of a possible encounter with aliens, according to a recent poll.

Controversy at Harvard

It is a quandary that polarizes researchers at Harvard University. One embattled psychiatrist, John Mack, M.D., argues that these experiences cannot be understood in a western rationalist tradition of science; researchers in the department of psychology, Richard McNally, Ph.D., and Susan Clancy, Ph.D., counter that the explanation—though multifaceted—is hilarious in its fundamental simplicity.

Mack, of Harvard Medical School, is a long-time champion of alien abductees and a paranormal philosopher king of sorts. His 1994 bestseller, *Abduction: Human Encounters With Aliens*, drew international attention with the argument that "experiencers," Mack's term for the men and women he has debriefed, probably are being abducted by aliens.

More recently, McNally and Clancy introduced alien abductees to the laboratory to study trauma and recovered memory in an experimental setting. They believe their subsequent findings explain the entire abduction experience, including abductees' refusal to accept the fact that transcendent, technicolor encounters with aliens are no more than five-alarm fires in the brain.

Harvard's ideological clashes over the interpretation of anomalous experiences date to William James' tenure at the university one century ago. Both Mack and James studied psychology after training in medicine and tried to bridge the gap between psychology and spirituality, only to be rebuffed by Harvard's powers that be. For James, this culminated in *Varieties of Religious Experience*, which rejected a rigorous standard of evidence for divine experiences. "There is a clinical literature and an experimental literature, and they don't refer to each other," states Eugene Taylor, Ph.D., a biographer of James and a historian who lectures on psychology at Harvard Medical School. "Mack is a clinician making observations about human experience, as opposed to cognitive behavioral scientists, who say that if you can't measure it in the laboratory, it doesn't exist." When it comes to people who believe they've been abducted by space aliens, the two camps agree on only one thing: "These people are almost never psychotic," says McNally. "They're not lying. But Mack entertains a range of explanations that are farfetched at best."

Traumatic Alien Encounters

Will Bueche, a 34-year-old media director, has long had nighttime paralysis and visions that "have no resolution and seem out of place." For years, he considered them merely suggestive—until he began witnessing beings while wide awake. Some abductees had far more traumatic encounters. Peter Faust, a 45-year-old acupuncturist, believes he endured years of sexual probing by hooded creatures who implanted chips in his anus and stimulated him to ejaculation. After eight hypnotic-regression sessions with Mack, and a battery of psychological tests in the early 1990s, Faust concluded that he is yoked to a female alien-human hybrid with whom he has multiple offspring.

The abduction narrative is a strange hybrid in its own right: humiliating surgical invasion tempered by cosmic awareness. Experiencers travel through windows and walls, tunnels and space-time to reach the starship's examining table, where young women's eggs are extracted and men's sperm are siphoned off. Despite waking bruised and violated, abductees say their love for beings in the alien realm can surpass any human bond and generate a sense of oceanic oneness with the universe that rivals the experiences of a world-class meditator. Faust says he "realized we're not alone in the universe. There are beings out there who care about us. But getting to this point is a long, arduous journey, with a lot of people who want to deny your experience."

Personality-driven explanations for why people with no overt psychopathology report alien encounters have proliferated apace with blockbuster movies about aliens. Psychologist Roy Baumeister, Ph.D., of Case Western Reserve University, argues that abduction reports are made by "masochists" who unconsciously want to relinquish control of their lives. The loss of control is manifest in humiliating encounters with an alien race. To be sure, there is a surfeit of elaborate sex in abduction reports; one study found that among abductees, 80 percent of women and 50 percent of men reported being examined naked on a table by humanoid beings. In fact, many abductees blame aliens for sexual dysfunction and emotional disturbances.

Psychologists have long surmised that abductees may be inclined to fantasy and "absorption," the propensity to daydream or be enthralled by novels. Both alien abductees and garden-variety fantasizers report false pregnancies, out-of-body experiences and apparition sightings. Some psychologists speculate that people like Will Bueche and Peter Faust are simply "encounter-prone" individuals with a heightened receptivity to anomalous experience. Whatever the case, Bueche and Faust found a willing listener in John Mack.

Dr. John Mack's Work

Mack has been on the faculty of Harvard Medical School since 1955, and in 1982 he founded the Center for Psychology and Social Change, located in a yellow clapboard house just beyond the university's campus. The Center aims in part to study anomalous experiences, and has its post office box in Cambridge, but the building lies just within neighboring Somerville. The address is a fitting line of demarcation for a clinician who straddled conventional science and altered states of consciousness long before the publication of *Abduction*.

Mack founded the department of psychiatry at The Cambridge Hospital in 1969; a program that has long attracted innovative, Eastern-oriented psychiatrists. In 1977, Mack was awarded a Pulitzer Prize for *A Prince of Our Disorder*, a biography of Lawrence of Arabia. "Mack is in dynamic communication with the humanities," says Eugene Taylor.

Mack has embraced traditions from Freudian psychoanalysis to the guided meditation of Werner Erhard. In 1988, he began to practice Stanislav Grof's holotropic breathwork, a technique that induces an altered state by means of deep, rapid breathing and evocative music. Mack believes he retrieved memories of his mother's death, which occurred when he was 8 months old. "I was raised in a tradition of inquiry," says Mack. "If you encounter something that doesn't fit your worldview, it's more intellectually honest to say, 'maybe there's something wrong with this worldview,' than to try to shoehorn your findings into an existing belief."

At 73, Mack appears regal despite his slightly stooped gait. His handsome, deeply lined face and flinty blue eyes are quietly compelling; he quickly earned a reputation for emotional succor among the abductees he interviewed. Abductees including Faust and Bueche cling to him like acolytes, often parroting his theories.

Mack used hypnotic regression to retrieve detailed memories of 13 encounters with aliens, all chronicled in *Abduction*. He has now interviewed more than 200 abductees. He says that he ultimately endorsed abduction reports largely because he found his subjects to be mentally competent. Some were also highly traumatized and most were reluctant to come forward and appropriately skeptical about their experiences.

Mack defends the use of controversial techniques such as hypnotic regression because he prizes the experiential narrative over empirical data. To debrief an abductee is to be "in the presence of a truth teller, a witness to a compelling, often sacred, reality." Mack says he was jolted when his subjects reported receiving telepathic warnings about man's decimation of natural resources. "I thought this was about aliens taking eggs and sperm and traumatizing people," admits Mack. "I was surprised to find it was an informational thing."

The faculty of Harvard Medical School, for its part, was dumbfounded that Mack believed he'd stumbled on anything more than an underreported cluster of psychiatric symptoms. From 1994 to 1995, Arnold Relman, M.D., professor emeritus of medicine, chaired an ad-hoc committee that conducted a 15-month investigation into Mack's work with abductees. "John did good things in his career and gained a lot of respect. His behavior with regard to the alien-abduction story disappointed a lot of his colleagues," says Relman. The investigation ended with much tongue-wagging but no formal censure. Mack was, however, encouraged to bring a multidisciplinary approach to his study of the phenomenon. "No one is challenging John's right to look into the matter," sighs Relman. "All we're saying is, if you do it, do it in an objective, scholarly manner."

The Possibility of Sleep Paralysis

In the spring of 1999, Mack invited astrophysicists, anthropologists and a Jungian analyst who studies anomalous experience in the wake of organ transplants to the Harvard Divinity School, where they brainstormed with mental health professionals and abductees. One participant was Harvard psychology professor Richard McNally, an expert on cognitive processing in anxiety disorders.

McNally told the assembly that "sleep-related aspects of the experiences might be correlated with different parts of the REM cycle." He was referring to the phenomenon of sleep paralysis, but he hesitated to speak bluntly about it. Many abductees deem sleep paralysis too mundane an explanation for their experiences, so McNally didn't use the term, for fear of "alienating" the very subjects he wanted to recruit.

Sleep paralysis is a common phenomenon—up to 60 percent of people have at least one episode, in which the brain and body momentarily desynchronize when waking from REM sleep. The body remains paralyzed, as is standard during the REM cycle, but the mind is semi-lucid or fully cognizant of its surroundings, even, according to a Japanese study, if one's eyes are closed. The experience can't be technically classified as either waking or sleeping. For an unlucky handful of people, fleeting paralysis is accompanied by horrifying visual and auditory hallucinations: bright lights, a sense of choking and the conviction that an intruder is present. The Japanese call it kanashibari, represented as a devil stepping on a hapless sleeper's chest; the Chinese refer to it as gui ya, or ghost pressure.

Sleep paralysis with hypnopompic hallucinations (those that occur upon waking) can be so unexpected and terrifying that people routinely believe they're stricken with a grave neurological illness or that they're going insane. When faced with these prospects, aliens no longer seem so nefarious.

But sleep paralysis and abduction don't always go hand in hand. . . . Why, then, do some people who experience violent hallucinations upon waking or falling asleep conclude that they have been abducted? One possibility is that people embellish their experience in the course of hypnotic regression. But McNally and Susan Clancy speculate that alien abductees aren't just amenable to suggestion under hypnosis; instead they actively create false memories. They drew this conclusion while studying one of the most contentious issues in psychology today: false memory syndrome.

False Memory Syndrome

The question of whether or not people repress traumatic memories was thrown into high relief 15 years ago, as psychotherapy patients increasingly recovered memories of sexual abuse, often through such porous techniques as hypnotic regression and guided imagery. Some cognitive psychologists, including McNally, argued that people rarely repress memories of abuse or trauma; if anything, they are more likely to recall the incident. Sexual-abuse victims remain silent "not because they are incapable of remembering, but because it's a terrible secret," says McNally. Other professionals argue that traumatic memories are easily repressed through specific dissociative mechanisms.

In 1996, McNally and Clancy became the first researchers to examine memory function in women who believed they had recovered memories of childhood sexual abuse. They found that these women were significantly more likely to create false memories of nontraumatic events in a lab than were women who had always remembered being sexually abused, or women who had never been abused. . . .

But McNally and Clancy could not ascertain whether the women had in fact been sexually abused. Since it is unethical to create false memories of trauma, the researchers did the next best thing: They amassed a group whose recovered memories were unlikely to have occurred. Those people were, of course, alien abductees.

McNally and Clancy assembled a group whose members believed they'd recovered memories (usually under hypnosis) of alien abduction, along with a repressed memory group whose members believed they'd been abducted but had no conscious memory of the event. (This group inferred their abduction from physical abrasions, waking in strange positions or sometimes just from their penchant for science fiction.) There was also a terrestrially bound control group who reported no abduction experiences.

The recovered and repressed memory groups exhibited high rates of false recall on [a] word-recognition test. Those with "intact" memories of abduction fared worse than those who believed their memories were repressed.

But could this type of false recall be a function of memory deficits incurred through traumatic experiences? No, says Clancy: "Real trauma survivors exhibit a broad range of memory impairments on this task. Recovered-memory survivors—whether the trauma is sexual abuse or alien abduction—exhibit just one impairment on this task: the tendency to create false memories."

False recall is a source-monitoring problem, an inability to remember where and when information is acquired: You think a friend told you a piece of news, for instance, but you actually heard it on the radio. "Human memory is not like a video recorder," says Clancy. "It's prone to distortion and decay over time. This does not mean that abductees are psychiatrically impaired. I don't think they should be considered weird. If anything, they're just more prone to creating false memories."

Subjects whose personality profiles indicated a high level of absorption or inclination to fantasy were the most likely to perform poorly on the word-recall task. Furthermore, says McNally, every abductee in the recovered memory group described what appears to be sleep paralysis.

Clancy and McNally outlined their findings in the *Journal of Abnormal Psychology* [in 2002], whittling the abduction phenomenon down to an equation of sorts. Susceptibility to creating false memories, coupled with a disturbing experience like sleep paralysis and a cultural script that allows for abduction by aliens, may lead one to falsely recall such an encounter. "You don't necessarily have to endorse these experiences to create false memories," says Clancy. "You may have just seen 'The X-Files' and thought, 'That's crap,' but then you have an episode of sleep paralysis that freaks you out, and the show is still in the back of your mind."

And among people wavering about whether or not they've been abducted, hypnosis can push them to embrace this interpretation. In a 1994 experiment that simulated hypnosis, psychologist Steven Jay Lynn asked subjects to imagine that they'd seen bright lights and experienced missing time. Ninety-one percent of those who'd been primed with questions about UFOs stated that they'd interacted with aliens.

Powerful Emotions

Still, if the abduction experience is a misinterpreted bout of sleep paralysis, why do abductees invest it with such emotion? A videotape of a tearful Peter Faust undergoing hypnotic regression is so powerful that Mack says he stopped showing the footage; it freaked out even nonabductees, causing many to erect "new defenses." Terror in the face of potentially false memories was one issue McNally hoped to study with abductees. This question brought him, in part, to the Divinity School conference. "I wanted to know whether people really have to be traumatized to produce a physiological reaction."

McNally collected testimony from 10 subjects with recovered memories of abduction then confronted them with the most frightening details of their own accounts—from violent trysts to swarms of aliens around their beds. Six out of 10 subjects registered such elevated physiological reactions, including heartbeat and facial muscle tension, that they met the criteria for posttraumatic stress disorder (PTSD).

Interestingly, subjects with PTSD react physiologically only to their own traumatic experiences, but the abductee group had heightened responses to additional stressful scripts, such as the violent death of a loved one. They even reacted to positive scripts, such as viewing their newborn infant for the first time. Such reactivity, coupled with high levels of absorption, has been linked to the ability to generate vivid imagery, according to McNally. In other words, abductees are more likely to experience a traumatic—or positive—scenario as real, in part due to their fertile imaginations. They will then react to it as such. "Emotion does not prove the veracity of the interpretation," McNally concludes.

For McNally, the most telling difference between abductees and survivors of "veritable" trauma is not physiological but attitudinal. Experiencers unanimously state that they're glad they were abducted. "There's a psychological payoff," says McNally. "This makes it very different from sexual abuse." Trauma survivors of all stripes cite positive spiritual growth, but, "no Vietnam vet says, 'Gee, I'm glad I was a POW.'"

It is understandable that memory lapses, as measured by poor performance on a lab test, pale in comparison to communication with unknown beings. And while abductees may feel assaulted by aliens, they also feel special. For that reason, "They are not trying to demystify their experience," says McNally, whose deconstruction of sleep paralysis for one woman was met with a polite smile and the exhortation that he should "think outside the box." When McNally finally broached the term "sleep paralysis" at Mack's conference, he says, "There was an awkward silence, as if someone had belched in church."

A Cross-Cultural Phenomenon

"I'm not personally interested in what Susan Clancy found," admits Bueche, for whom the memory test was "50 bucks and free Chinese food." I don't need evidence or proof. Most experiencers are well beyond that. This is about what you can learn regardless of whether it is physically real or interdimensional or something grand that the mind is generating."

Mack counters that no combination of sleep paralysis and the Sci-Fi Channel explains phenomena such as alien sightings by school children in Zimbabwe who are wide-awake. "It doesn't even come close," he says. Mack's second book, *Passport to the Cosmos*, chronicles abduction as a cross-cultural phenomenon; he finds evidence of sexual and ecological parallels to American abduction reports on almost every continent.

Mack . . . increasingly distances himself from the question of whether or not aliens exist in the physical world, focusing more on a "consensus reality" that precludes us from even entertaining such a possibility. "We void the cosmos of other intelligence unless it can be proven," states Mack. On the work of McNally and Clancy in the psychology department, a stone's throw away, Mack says, "We're in different firmaments."

Speculation That Ancient Astronauts Shaped Humankind Is Not New

Donna Kossy

Donna Kossy specializes in researching beliefs that aren't accepted by mainstream science. One chapter of her book *Strange Creations* is about the theory that extraterrestrials came to Earth in the past and influenced early civilizations. Unlike most critics of this belief, who emphasize its conflict with facts established by archaeology, Kossy focuses on how and why it arose. Although people often assume it is based on new discoveries or scholarly research, Kossy maintains that it actually grew out of an old esoteric tradition and has since been promoted to the general public through books by non-scholars that became best sellers. The full chapter of *Strange Creations* provides many details about books on "ancient astronauts" that preceded those of the currently popular writers Erich von Däniken and Zecharia Sitchin. In the following selection from it, Kossy explains where these two writers got their ideas.

One of the best-known aberrant anthropologies—often touted as the middle ground between creationism and evolution—is the "alien intervention" theory of human origins. This theory—or family of theories—is well summarized by authors Max Flindt and Otto Binder in their 1974 book *Mankind: Child of the Stars.* "Starmen visited Earth," they wrote, "and mated with early females (perhaps hominids) to sire the modern human race of *Homo sapiens.*" Upon discovery of this theory during a surge of UFO popularity in the 1970s, it struck me as instantly appealing and exciting. Not only might we humans come in contact with extraterrestrial beings, but ETs might actually be our ancestors, or maybe even our brothers: we ourselves could be "star people."

This entertaining theory, which seems tailor-made for the space age, is not as new as it might seem. On the one hand, it updates the old creation myths that depict human beings as the children or creation of sky gods—only the "sky gods" are advanced extraterrestrial beings who colonized Earth and created mankind via experiments in genetic engineering or by interbreeding (themselves) with terrestrial ape creatures. On the other hand, the ET theory's true roots lie in Western esotericism and nineteenth century Theosophy.

New Life to an Old Myth

The belief that men and women descended from (or were created by) space gods stems from neither science nor organized religion, but a third, esoteric tradition. This tradition and its practices go by various names: esotericism, occultism, gnosticism, spiritualism, Theosophy, and, most often, the New Age. Like organized religion, esotericism acknowledges an unseen world, but unlike organized religion, it invites direct participation in it. Rather than place themselves, permanently, far below the level of the all-powerful creator-spirit, esotericists seek to ascend to the level of the gods, to experience spirituality first-hand, to contact invisible entities, even to influence the cosmos. . . .

Even though the esotericists are seriously interested in spiritual matters, they are often alienated from traditional, organized religion. At the same time, they distrust scientific theories because those theories are devoid of spiritual meaning. Modern participants in the "unseen world" believe that the role of the human being in the cosmos is more than just as a complex, accidental animal or a lowly servant of a jealous creator. To them, men and women are vital players in a grand, cosmic drama. So, naturally, they are attracted to myths that depict humanity as the children or creation of space gods. . . .

Sky People and Space Brothers

Before the first "flying saucer" appeared in 1947, sky people and angels dwelt in the spirit world, their "bodies" made of an entirely different, "lighter" substance than physical bodies in the material world. By the late 1940s, however, a new generation began to identify sky people and even God Himself as simply "men of other planets." The veil of mystery was being removed in everything from electricity to deadly disease, so why not remove the mystery from spirits and gods as well? It would be safe to believe in the gods again—even in the nuts-and-bolts worshipping twentieth century—if they were simply extraterrestrials who were not too different from human beings. "Flying saucer contactees" began receiving visits from "saucer men" much like mystics receive visits from spirits or angels. Cosmic tutors in the guise of kindly extraterrestrials or "space brothers" began meeting with selected members of our human tribe, providing sorely needed philosophical tutelage on such urgent topics as nuclear war and the fate of the human race. Nobody seemed to notice, however, that they had traveled all that way to impart information gleaned just as easily from the Bible or [theosophist H.P. Blavatsky's] Secret Doctrine.

In 1953, *Flying Saucers Have Landed* by British novelist and musician Desmond Leslie (born 1921) and American contactee George Adamski (1891–1965) became an overnight best-seller. Adamski, who had taught what he called the "Universal Laws" since the 1930s, claimed to have seen flying saucers with his own eyes. Leslie, however—as he told a Detroit flying saucer club in 1954—hadn't given flying saucers much thought until his publisher asked him to write a science fiction story about them. While researching the story, the young author concluded that flying saucers were, in fact, real. The resulting nonfiction book, *Flying Saucers Have Landed*, was a landmark, eventually translated into 16 languages. Adamski detailed his encounter with Venusians in the Mojave Desert, while Leslie broke new ground with his discussion of ancient astronauts.

Not only were spacemen visiting Earth now, suggested Leslie, but they have been landing on our planet for millennia. The first saucer landing (from Venus) took place around 19 million B.C. Extraterrestrials have left thousands of artifacts since ancient times, including Stonehenge and the Egyptian pyramids; they have also inspired myths and legends, including the story of Ezekiel's Wheel from the Bible. These claims were soon repeated by other authors. Leslie seems to have been the first, however, to ask how ancient peoples could have achieved such difficult feats is moving the blocks of Stonehenge without help from space people. Best-selling authors *still* haven't stopped repeating that question.

Updating an Old Message

Leslie also addressed the question of human origins, updating and simplifying Blavatsky's story in *The Secret Doctrine* for the postwar audience. The Hindu *Puranas*, wrote Leslie, "contain records, in allegorical form, of Universal Man's ceaseless pilgrimage through space." According to these ancient documents, human seeds arrive on each new planet, and then grow up through the mineral, vegetable, animal and human kingdoms, and ultimately the kingdom of God. At the end of each planetary cycle, the hidden God within humanity emerges and "the seeds are gathered up and taken through space in immense shining ships to the next planet for development." Leslie called such ships "Interplanetary Noah's Arks.". . .

Though this kind of information might have been new to teenaged UFO buffs, it was old hat to students of Theosophy, since Leslie's message drew overtly from *The Secret Doctrine*. Meanwhile, Adamski's Venusians spoke of the same "Universal Laws" he had been pushing since the '30s. In his first book, *Wisdom of the Masters of the Far East* (1936), "Professor G. Adamski" revealed secret teachings of the "Royal Order of Tibet." Later, after he'd encountered flying saucers, the contactee penciled in "Space Brothers" wherever he'd written "Royal Order of Tibet.". . .

The contactees in the 1950s, and then [Max] Flindt, in 1962, were among the first to discover the ancient astronauts as symbolic of the fusion between science and spirit. But it wasn't until the late '60s and early '70s that "ancient astronauts" would become a household phrase.

In 1969, Erich von Däniken's mass market paperback, *Chariots of the Gods?*, published in Germany the previous year, blanketed the United States. In the traditions of Desmond Leslie and [*Flying Saucer Review* editor] Brinsley LePoer Trench, von Däniken saw "ancient astronauts" as responsible for every earthly mystery from Ezekiel's Wheel to the Mayan and Egyptian Pyramids to the enigma of our own existence. Sales of this blockbuster approached 50 million copies. I personally remember the book provoking many heated debates in my high school cafeteria. Von Däniken was obviously touching a nerve that went far beyond the saucer clubs and space brother contactees.

Von Däniken's Search for the Gods

Erich von Däniken was born in Zofingen, Switzerland in 1935 and was raised in a strict, Catholic household. He often butted heads with his pious father and with his teachers at the Jesuit College of Saint-Michel (a secondary school) in Fribourg, Switzerland. His father removed him from the school after he had completed only three years there. Von Däniken then began a career as hotelier, working his way up from cook and waiter to manager. But his real passion lay elsewhere. After hours, von Däniken would devote himself to archeology, astronomy and metaphysics.

Von Däniken's search for "the gods" began when he first experienced the paranormal in 1954, at age 19. He later told *Der Spiegel* magazine that ESP was "a source which led me to the firm belief that the earth had been visited by extraterrestrial astronauts." In the ESP experiences, "one makes a sort of 'journey through time.' I step out of time, so I stand outside time and see everything simultaneously—past, present, and future."

In 1966 the starry-eyed hotel manager finished his first book, *Memories of the Future*, the result of late-night sessions until three and four in the morning. The following year, von Däniken's book—out of all the thousands of amateurs in search of a publisher—was accepted by Econ-Verlag. In March of 1968, after extensive rewriting by Wilhelm Roggersdorf, a film producer and screenwriter, the first 6,000 copies of *Memories of the Future* were printed. The book was an unqualified hit. The next year it was published and renamed *Chariots of the Gods?* in West Germany and became that country's number one best-seller.

While von Däniken was still toiling away as a hotel manager, he began spending his vacations in Egypt, Lebanon and America to see the ancient astronaut evidence himself. In order to finance his journeys, however, he had to embezzle over 400,000 Swiss francs. In 1968, as his book was climbing the best-seller lists, he was arrested for fraud.

In court, he pleaded that this behavior was justified by the scholar's impassioned quest for knowledge. But the judges were not convinced, and in 1970 von Däniken was convicted of embezzlement, fraud and forgery. His sentence was three and a half years in prison and a fine of 3,000 francs. This sum was easily paid off by his ever-growing royalty checks, and he was let out of prison early. Free of legal entanglements, now the budding author could fulfill his dream of devoting himself to ancient astronauts full time. Von Däniken is still churning out sequels, 30 years later.

An Alien Breeding Experiment?

In *Chariots of the Gods?* von Däniken attributed artifacts and monuments such as the Great Pyramid of Cheops and the markings on the Plain of Nazca in Peru—and humanity itself—to ancient astronauts. In the chapter entitled "Was God an Astronaut?" he asks another question: "Does not [evidence from the Bible] seriously pose the question whether the human race is not an act of deliberate 'breeding' by unknown beings from outer space?" He later suggested a scenario that was old hat to the flying saucer buffs but seemed daring to the uninitiated:

> Dim, as yet undefinable ages ago an unknown spaceship discovered our planet. Obviously the "man" of those times was no *Homo sapiens* but something rather different. The spacemen artificially fertilized some female members of this species, put them into a deep sleep, so ancient legends say, and departed. Thousands of years later the space travelers returned and found scattered specimens of the genus *Homo sapiens*. . . .

Von Däniken's version of humanity as an alien breeding experiment, like those that came before, loosely follows the Bible. Like Blavatsky's narrow-headed Lemurians and [George] Van Tassel's alien-beast hybrids, some of Adam's genetically altered progeny were unable to control themselves, and continued to mate with animals. This "backsliding" represented the Fall of Man because it "impeded evolution," and retained the bestial in man. A few thousand years later, however, presumably at the time of Noah's flood, the cosmonauts corrected this situation. "They destroyed the hybrid animal-men, separated a well-preserved group of new men, and implanted new genetic material in them by a second artificial mutation."

Though derivative of earlier authors, von Däniken was able to reach those who had never touched a flying saucer book in their lives. After the appearance of *Chariots of the Gods?* the idea that spacemen created humanity as a genetic experiment was circulating in perhaps 50 million minds. . . . After von Däniken and others cleared the field for speculation in this vein, the market was flooded with reinterpretations of the Bible as an extraterrestrial epic.

The Raëlian Movement

Von Däniken wasn't the only European to popularize ancient astronauts during the late '60s. In 1968, French author Jean Sendy, who had previously written on biblical and occult subjects, came out with a new title, *La Lune, Cle de la Bible*. It was translated as *The Moon: Outpost of the Gods* for U.S. distribution in 1975. In this book Sendy, like Brinsley LePoer Trench before him, suggested that the biblical book of Genesis is a literal account of the coming of extraterrestrial colonists to Earth, known biblically as Elohim.

Five years later, on December 13, 1973, Sendy's disclosure of the true identity of the Elohim was dramatically confirmed by auto racing journalist Claude Vorilhon; he spoke to an extraterrestrial who emerged from a hovering spaceship in a dormant volcano in the French countryside. A small humanoid in a green suit told Vorilhon that he had come from "a far distant planet" similar to Earth "to observe the evolution of human beings and to watch over them." He had chosen Vorilhon specifically to be his messenger, and his new name would be Raël. . . .

Räel learned that scientists from the ET's planet had come to Earth long ago to conduct experiments in creating life, and that the word "Elohim" from the Bible, when properly translated, means "those who came from the sky." The humanoid explained that the line, "And the spirit of Elohim moved across the waters" in Genesis 1:2, really means, "[The extraterrestrials] made reconnaissance flights, and what you might call artificial satellites were placed around the earth to study its constitution and atmosphere." Likewise, the true story behind the line "Elohim saw that the light was good" in Genesis 1:4, is, "To create life on Earth it was important to know whether the sun was sending harmful rays to the earth's surface."

The Elohim, of course, also created mankind, but it wasn't until August 6, 1945, the day the United States dropped the atomic bomb on Hiroshima, that humanity had finally "reached the stage in its scientific evolution where it was now ready to understand the truth about its origins." And now that we know the truth, the Elohim are imploring us, through Raël, to welcome them back to Earth by building an embassy for them in Jerusalem. It is up to the International Raëlian Movement to spread the Elohim's messages, to build the embassy and to prepare humanity for their imminent arrival.

The Raëlian movement claims over 30,000 members in 67 countries; the messages of the Elohim have been translated into 19 languages. This classic New Age religion embraces sensual practices and meditations inspired by Eastern religion, as well as a religious philosophy which updates the standard Judeo-Christian mythology with space-age technology. The Raëlians are overtly opposed, however, to the scientific establishment and regard evolution by "chance" as a "myth." They embrace technological progress while rejecting the scarier atheist under-pinnings of science.

Pseudo-Scholarly Blockbusters

During the ancient astronaut boom in the '70s, Zecharia Sitchin's 1976 offering, *The 12th Planet*, almost got lost in the shuffle. Twenty years later, however, Sitchin became heir to von Däniken's block-buster kingdom. During the '90s, Sitchin's series of best-selling pseudo-scholarly books have fostered a huge and fanatical following. While his fans believe the author's claim to scholarly credentials, his actual scientific understanding is limited, at best. Sitchin may be, as he insists, an expert in ancient languages, but his greatest expertise is his ability to twist the logic of modern languages. Yet people who would laugh at von Däniken or Van Tassel are beguiled by the schol-arly bait-and-switch of Zecharia Sitchin.

Sitchin was born in 1920 in Baku in the former USSR, later emigrat-ing to England and then Israel. Before delving into the arcane field of extraterrestrial intervention, Sitchin served in the British and Israeli Armies and then distinguished himself in journalism, foreign trade and public service. . . .

Sitchin claims, as well, to be an "expert" in ancient languages, trained at Hebrew University in Jerusalem. However, the biographical source I checked lists his only degree as Bachelor of Commerce (B.Com.) from the University of London. Aside from his membership in various museum and Oriental societies, there is no mention of any scholarly credentials; his most obvious talents are promotion and marketing.

Sitchin adds the pretense of expertise to standard ancient astronaut lore. His chains of argument, however, are as flawed as von Däniken's. He frequently points to ancient illustrations, claiming they depict rockets, batteries, helmets and electronic devices used by people who lived thousands of years ago. Yet he never wonders why archeologists haven't yet found any hi-tech equipment buried in the rubble of the ancient cities.

Sitchin's fans perceive him as an original thinker. But his hallmark, interpreting battles between gods in Sumerian texts as collisions be-tween planets, is nothing new. In the early '50s, George Hunt Williamson used arguments based on made-up word associations that Sitchin would perfect later; he identified the Babylonian god Marduk with an extra planet called "Maldek"—an idea that was a direct pre-cursor to Sitchin's *12th Planet*.

Sitchin's View of Humankind's Origin

In the *12th Planet*, Sitchin claims to read the Sumerian *Epic of Creation* (a work we can assume is unfamiliar to much of his audience) at "face value." At face value, the tale is one of the creation of the waters, heavens and earth by gods. Sitchin, however, reads it as tale about the peregrinations of planetary bodies. Sitchin provides bits and pieces of the epic, but he never summarizes the original story in full. If he did, his argument would fall apart. . . .

Marduk, according to Sitchin, is the home planet of our creators, an intelligent, humanoid race he calls the "Nefilim.". . . . The word "Nefilim" comes not from Sumerian, but from Genesis 6:4, "The Nefilim were upon the earth, in those days and thereafter too, when the sons of the gods cohabited with the daughters of the Adam, and they bore children unto them. They were the mighty ones of Eternity—The People of the *Shem*." *Shem*, usually translated as "name" or "reputation," Sitchin identifies as "fiery rocket." In defense of this strange translation, Sitchin employs von Däniken-style arguments based on how much all those ancient artifacts seem to depict rockets and space helmets and airports. Hence, the Nefilim are the "people of the fiery rockets.". . .

Sitchin returns to the *Epic of Creation* for the story of the creation of mankind. Only now the "gods," whom he'd previously interpreted as "planets," transform magically into extraterrestrials from Marduk; . . . The Nefilim and "their chief scientist, Ea," created *Homo sapiens* to be [a] primitive worker by genetically manipulating the most advanced human at the time, *Homo erectus.* . . .

Sitchin, true to the ancient astronaut credo, tells us that humanity is a hybrid between evolved hominids and advanced extraterrestrials, while providing a vague critique of Darwin. He wonders, "Are we really nothing more than 'naked apes'?" "No!" he answers. Darwinian evolution is correct, but only up to a point. When it identifies humanity as an accident that befell a band of apes, he's forced to bail out. Like almost every author discussed in this chapter, he asserts that "evolution can explain the general course of events that caused life on Earth, but evolution cannot account for the appearance of *Homo sapiens.*" Instead, he finds it more likely that humankind was genetically engineered as a slave for extraterrestrial gold miners.

Obviously, Sitchin's popularity comes not from the strength of his arguments. He's more concerned with "proving" his alternative history by bending the available evidence than with altering his theory to fit the facts. Like von Däniken, he has tapped into the imagination of the popular mind which is disillusioned and distrustful of hard science, even while embracing many of its accomplishments.

A Lack of Imagination

Ironically, Sitchin's interpretations of myth are embedded in a stubborn materialism usually identified with science. To Sitchin, myths don't depict anything spiritual or intangible at all; they depict only hard, historic events. Ea wasn't the god of wisdom; he was the god of mining. Though Sitchin's conclusion seem imaginative, they stem from a *lack* of imagination shared with some fundamentalists, an inability to connect with the cosmos and its mysteries in any but the most literal way.

Many of Sitchin's followers come from the New Age tradition, which sees humanity as something more than just a particularly successful genotype. Blavatsky, the spiritualists, the flying saucer contactees and current esoteric believers all maintain that our culture's sacred texts, including the Bible, are *not* incorrect, just incorrectly interpreted. The human race was created by powerful beings, after all—extraterrestrials to whom we are inextricably and genetically linked.

BOTH SCIENTISTS AND UFOLOGISTS NEED OPEN MINDS

David Grinspoon

David Grinspoon is a principal scientist in the Department of Space Studies at the Southwest Research Institute and adjunct professor of astrophysical and planetary sciences at the University of Colorado. He lectures frequently and maintains a Web site, www.funkyscience.net, where many of his articles on extraterrestrial life can be found. The following selection expresses his belief that because both scientists and ufologists (researchers who study the UFO phenomenon) start from arbitrary assumptions about extraterrestrials, they should be more tolerant of each others' views than they have been in the past. The selection comes from his book *Lonely Planets: The Natural Philosophy of Alien Life*, which won the PEN Center USA's 2004 Literary Award for Research Nonfiction.

It seems to me that [UFO] events are not as easy to explain away as the debunkers would like to believe. The skeptics may even be doing something they often accuse their "opponents" of: avoiding the truth out of fear of the unknown. You can come up with a rational explanation for anything. This doesn't mean that your theory is correct, but its mere existence can be comforting. . . .

There are some mysteries. Are we being unpatriotic to the flag of science if we admit there are some mysteries?

Too Much Debunking?

Some ufologists do attempt to apply rigorous methods to documenting strange phenomena seen in the sky. But they are up against an awful lot, including the rest of ufology, and we scientists don't usually talk to them. Many of us have had bad experiences with aggressive ufologists accusing us of all kinds of nasty things for not taking their ideas seriously.

If we are being honest, then our scientific attempts to debunk UFOs must contain caveats. This doesn't mean that debunking false reports is not worthwhile. Indeed, it is essential if we are ever going to be able to recognize the real thing. But sometimes we forget that we don't really know much about aliens. Unfortunately, the skeptics' attitude toward UFOs often has a moralizing tone, justified by a concern that the masses will turn back to medieval darkness if we don't wake them up by shining the spotlight of science right in their faces. . . .

The most extreme UFO believers and debunkers are caught in a feedback loop in which each side validates the other's existence. Overzealous efforts to discredit UFO reports help to reinforce the wide perception of scientific skepticism as intolerant and narrow-minded. Believers accuse debunkers of being in on a conspiracy, which leads to more hysterical debunking, and so on.

Debunking, unfortunately, must be done case by case. Unfortunately, there are a lot of cases. . . . Why can't we do a mass debunking? Some attempts have been made, but many of the arguments are quite weak. They generally amount to "If they are real aliens, why don't they act as we would expect aliens to act?" and rest on assumptions about the nature of alien technology, society, motivations, and so on. In some cases, the skeptics, just like the believers, have clearly made up their minds in advance. Each community is quite sure it is saving the world from the other.

The whole debunking concept, when applied to other people's belief systems, as opposed to specific reports of events or phenomena, is antiproductive. It doesn't lead to greater understanding. The term itself does not connote an effort to win over or convince those who don't agree with you. It's meant to show them to be the idiots they really are. "Your beliefs are bunk" is a trifle condescending.

Some people who see themselves on the science side of a science/anti-science divide develop their own strain of credulity, accepting anything published with the stamp of scientific approval as automatically authentic. Organized skepticism is always in danger of an ironic slide into its own form of dogmatism. The UFO debunkers know what they expect to find. This makes me think twice about debunking reports. After I think twice, I usually agree with them. Much debunking of specific claims has been done carefully, thoroughly, and convincingly. But many scientists do have a strong ideological commitment to keeping UFO reports within a certain class of phenomenon. If a UFO report turned out to be evidence of actual alien spacecraft, and aliens who do not follow our rules, a frightening tear would be rent in the fabric of our worldview.

Questioning Established Views

I grew up hearing a lot about UFOs from my parents and their friends, and from reading [science fiction authors Isaac] Asimov and [Arthur C.] Clarke and communing with the science fiction crowd—all people who loved to think about alien life and space travel, and who would have welcomed real alien contact more enthusiastically than anyone else. Yet the dominant view was that UFO believers were generally quite deluded.

That is not a controversial statement even among UFO believers, most of whom seem eager to distance themselves from those *other* UFO believers, whom they regard as *really* flaky. But are all of them deluded? [Astronomer Carl] Sagan and Asimov and my dad thought the answer was yes.

They were my authorities and one of their commandments was to question authority. So I had to question them, even while questioning whether this was always a good idea. At various times I've forced myself to rethink my stance on UFOs. Not wanting to just form my opinion based on authority, or received knowledge, I've had to ask myself if we might all somehow be deceived on this issue.

Science says, "Without objectively verifiable evidence, assume that it doesn't exist." But it is more accurate to say, "Without such evidence, we can't say whether it exists." We must be careful not to become lazy and let our skeptical mind-set become a closed one.

We have a certain view of how aliens will and will not behave and manifest their presence here. We get huffy when these imagined rules of interplanetary etiquette (of necessity based on projections of ourselves) are not followed. Skeptics complain that the aliens reported by UFO enthusiasts don't act like real aliens. Real aliens would not spend that kind of money on space fuel (energy is money). They'd stay home and improve things in their own systems. Real aliens wouldn't be interested in kidnapping humans and examining us or stealing sperm and eggs. We can't think of any good reason for them to behave like that. Real aliens would surely leave some spare parts or trash or footprints behind for us to study. Don't you know *anything* about aliens?

Yet, science faces some special challenges in applying itself to the question of intelligent aliens. Our methodology and philosophy assume that nature doesn't care about and isn't aware of our experiments. (Some ufologists assume the opposite.) We don't really know how to study something that knows it is being studied or might not want to be studied, or that *might even be studying us*. All our standards of evidence and proof—repeatability, multiple witnesses, material evidence, and so on—might fail with something that is actively messing with our minds, aware of us, and being careful *not* to be of interest to mainstream science.

What If Humans Were Being Studied?

Imagine for a moment that aliens were aware of our scientific method and were careful not to reveal themselves, perhaps out of compassion. You could envision their rules for avoiding our scrutiny:

Memo to All Space Brothers: Remember that human contact

is to be avoided whenever possible. They are stuck in the "science" phase we went through eons before we went intergalactic. We can use this to predict their reactions and avoid suspicion. Under no circumstances leave any physical evidence that could be used to scientifically deduce our existence and extraterrestrial origin. It's inevitable that humans will occasionally detect our activities, and this is acceptable as long as they don't have what they consider to be a "scientific" case. So if you are detected, make absolutely sure that the observation is not replicable, and keep your spectral scramblers on. Such occasional cases are puzzling to them and help maintain our secrecy by sowing doubt about all sightings.

Science has given us criteria for distinguishing the physical from the metaphysical. But if a conscious entity is studying us, which box does it go in? If advanced technology is indistinguishable from magic, the boundary between the physical and the metaphysical vanishes again, as if science never happened.

Arguments Depend on Assumptions

Are SETI aliens, fashioned from logical scientific extrapolations, more likely to be realistic than UFO aliens who don't follow our rules? Not necessarily. Despite the undeniable truth of Clarke's Third Law ["any sufficiently advanced technology is indistinguishable from magic"], in our debunking of alien stories we insist that aliens must conform to our current notions of evolution, our current understanding of the laws of physics, and some extrapolation of our own technological capabilities. Because we must extrapolate from the known, and because we cannot consider to be real any phenomenon for which there is no scientifically acceptable evidence, we are not open to magic. So scientists may not be any better qualified than anyone else to predict what aliens will be like.

Here's what we don't always cop to: Our scientific arguments against "the extraterrestrial hypothesis" for UFOs depend on a framework of assumptions. These are the pesky metaphysical leaks and leaps in our airtight worldview—the things we feel we know to be true, but cannot prove.

It wouldn't hurt our credibility to acknowledge that science has its own superstitions. We assume the existence of an objective reality that is independent from our consciousness. We assume that our minds do not create or affect what we observe. We also assume nature is consistent and repeatable, and therefore knowable. In all of this I could replace "we assume" with "I believe." I don't doubt any of this. This set of regulations for nature seems so obvious and reasonable to me that it almost seems absurd to question it. But if you dig down deep beneath our solid tower of reason, deduction, and provisional truth, you see that the whole thing is planted in loose sand, supported by received, or intuitively perceived, knowledge.

I'm a believer because this is the way the world seems. Further, I think that most everyone knows that this is the way it is. You can spin intellectual counterarguments to your heart's content, or you can meditate your way clear out of the galactic disk, but on your way back home tonight notice how your every move, breath, and thought is steeped in a solid world of consistent phenomena. If this is an illusion, I don't think we can shake it. . . . No matter what you believe, reality is something that we directly perceive, and we all operate on the experiential understanding that the world has external, material solidity.

Much as we "real alien researchers" would like the UFO phenomenon to just go away, we can't dismiss all UFO reports out of hand. We might miss something important. Further, we alienate a large segment of the public when we appear to be closed-minded, snotty, and overconfident.

Scientists and Ufologists Have Much in Common

In general it doesn't really bother me what people believe. I care more about how people behave toward one another, and some of the nicest people I've met have also seemed to have had some of the wackiest ideas. UFO believers and SETI scientists reject each other's philosophy, but both rely on the same core argument from plenitude. It's still the best justification for the existence of aliens: With so many stars and planets, there just has to be other intelligent life. Why should we be the only ones? You will hear this exact same logic and sentiment trumpeted from the stage at conferences of both ufology and astrobiology.

I've found something else that scientists and ufologists have in common, something wonderful that is widespread among diverse communities with vastly different approaches toward alien life: a sense of humor. Certainly, some take themselves and their beliefs too seriously, but there is wide recognition, on all sides, of the absurdity of the subject matter, and an ability to laugh about it. This could be a good starting place for scientists and ufologists to meet. If I ever ran a joint SETI/UFO conference, inviting a constructive dialogue between skeptics and believers, I would make the first and last session of every day a comedy session.

CHAPTER 4

WHAT WOULD EXTRATERRESTRIAL CONTACT MEAN TO HUMANKIND?

Contemporary Issues
Companion

Success in SETI Would Have Positive Benefits

Allen Tough

In 1999, an international seminar was held in Hawaii to discuss the potential impact that contact with a highly advanced intelligence will have on human civilization. Sponsored by the Foundation for the Future, it was attended by sixteen experts on the topic and coordinated by Allen Tough of the University of Toronto, who specializes in study of issues that affect the long-range future of humankind and is particularly knowledgeable about SETI. The following selection comes from Dr. Tough's introduction to the seminar report, in which he summarizes the positive benefits that many scientists, including the majority of the seminar participants, expect might result from contact with advanced extraterrestrials.

Contact with intelligent life from somewhere else in our galaxy will probably occur sometime in humanity's future. It might take the form of a richly detailed radio or laser message from the distant civilization, for instance, or a super-intelligent probe that reaches our planet. Such contact might occur next year, or 20 or 30 years from now, or not for 100 years, or even longer.

Few events in the entire sweep of human history would be as significant and far-reaching, affecting our deepest beliefs about the nature of the universe, our place in it, and what lies ahead for human civilization. Seeking contact and preparing for successful interaction should be two of the top priorities on our civilization's current agenda.

Such contact will surely be an extraordinary event in all of human history. Over the next thousand years, several significant events will, no doubt, have a powerful, positive impact on human society. But making contact with another civilization will likely be the event with the highest positive impact of all. . . .

Any other civilizations in our galaxy are probably much older than human civilization. Two factors support this assumption. First, the vast majority of stars in our galaxy are much older than our Sun, many of them millions of years older. It follows, then, that any civilizations on planets revolving around those stars likely arose much earlier than our own civilization did. Second, it seems quite possible that some civilizations survive for a million years or even longer. If the civilizations in our galaxy range in age from a few thousand years up to a million years, then we are one of the youngest: by most definitions, human civilization is not much more than 10,000 years old.

Because other civilizations in our galaxy are thousands of years older than human civilization, they have probably advanced in certain ways beyond our present level of development. Some civilizations presumably fail to survive once they discover nuclear weapons or other means of causing their own extinction, but surely others learn to cope successfully with such problems and then survive for a very long time. Some of them may be 100,000 years or even millions of years more advanced than we are. . . .

SETI has not yet succeeded in detecting any repeatable evidence. But the range of strategies and the intensity of the efforts are growing rapidly, making success all the more likely in the next few decades. More than one strategy may succeed, of course, so that by the year 3000 we may well be engaged in dialogue with several different civilizations (or other forms of intelligence) that originated in various parts of our Milky Way galaxy.

The Long-Term Perspective

Because of our society's focus on the immediate present and on the very short-term future, it is difficult to switch into a long-term perspective. As a result, most oral and printed discussions of contact focus on the immediate and short-term effects. In contrast, right from the beginning, my vision of this seminar emphasized the long-term perspective. . . . [This was] because of the major differences between short-term and long-term effects of contact. The short-term effects are likely to be chaotic, frenzied, unsettling—perhaps marked by resistance and conflict, by extreme media reactions, and by political maneuvering or even warfare (military or covert). Although these effects are very important for the SETI field to study and prepare for, they are not the focus of this particular seminar. If handled well, presumably most of these short-term effects will fade within a few years. Our discussion here will focus on the potential effects on human civilization several decades or centuries after contact occurs.

If SETI succeeds, two types of contact are possible. One possibility is simply evidence that another advanced intelligence exists somewhere in the universe, with little information about its characteristics and no dialogue. One example is evidence of a . . . major astroengineering project many light-years away, with no additional information about its creators. Another example is a radio message that arrives from many light-years away but is not successfully decoded even after many years of effort.

The second possibility is contact that yields a rich storehouse of knowledge about the extraterrestrial intelligence and its history, technology, science, values, social organization, and so on. This could occur through an encyclopedic radio or optical message that we manage to decode. Because of recent progress in nanotechnology, artificial intelligence, and space exploration, we now realize that closeup contact with a small but super-smart probe is at least as likely a scenario. In fact, by monitoring our telecommunications, the probe will likely have learned our languages and be able to communicate with us quite effectively: no decoding necessary! . . .

Our discussion will assume that some sort of major information exchange or lively back-and-forth dialogue occurs between humans and some form of extraterrestrial intelligence. The particular scenario is not important . . . ; it could be a rapidly translated encyclopedic message sent from 40 light-years away by radio or laser, for instance, or a small but extraordinarily intelligent probe sent by a civilization with technology 100,000 years ahead of ours. . . .

Five Sorts of Contact

This report examines five sorts of long-term consequences that could result from contact. . . .

1. Practical Information.

We might well receive practical information and advice that helps our human civilization to survive and flourish. Possible examples include technology, transportation, a new form of energy, a new way of producing food or nourishing ourselves, a feasible solution to population growth, more effective governance and social organization, fresh views on values and ethics, and inspiration to shift direction dramatically in order to achieve a reasonably positive future. The message might also bring home to people the importance of eliminating warfare or at least eliminating weapons of extraordinary destruction. Viewing ourselves from an extraterrestrial perspective might be very useful in reducing our emphasis on differences and divisions among humans, and instead seeing ourselves as one human family.

2. Answers to Major Questions.

We might gain new insights and knowledge about deep, major questions that go far beyond ordinary practical day-to-day matters. Topics in an encyclopedia-like message or closeup dialogue could include astrophysics, the origin and evolution of the universe, religious questions, the meaning and purpose of life, and answers to philosophical questions. We might receive detailed information about the other civilization (which might be deeply alien to us) and about its philosophies and beliefs. Similar information could be provided about several other civilizations throughout our galaxy, too. We might even receive a body of knowledge accumulated over the past billion years through contributions by dozens of civilizations throughout the galaxy.

What sorts of consequences will contact have for our religious ideas and institutions? Some religions may be deeply shaken by contact, or at least need to reexamine their set of beliefs. It seems clear, however, that humanity's religions have already flourished over many centuries despite a variety of scientific discoveries that conflict with religious views. And several religions have already incorporated the idea of extraterrestrial life. Although some religious leaders may denounce an extraterrestrial dialogue, most will surely embrace it as further evidence of God's infinite greatness.

3. Changes in Our View of Ourselves.

Richly detailed information from an extraterrestrial civilization might transform our view of ourselves and our place in the universe, even our ultimate destination. We might gain a much deeper sense of ourselves as part of intelligent life and evolving culture throughout the universe—or at least part of a galactic family of civilizations. We might develop a deeper sense of meaning and connectedness to a universe filled with biology and intelligence. A new cosmotheology or global/cosmic ethic might arise, or a powerful secular movement of altruistic service to the universe and its long-term flourishing. . . .

[Foreign Service officer] Michael Michaud pointed out 22 years ago that "contact would be immensely broadening and deprovincializing. It would be a quantum jump in our awareness of things outside ourselves. It would change our criteria of what matters. We would have to think in interstellar, even galactic frames of reference. We would leave the era of Earth history, and enter an era of cosmic history."

In *The SETI Factor*, Frank White raised the possibility that SETI "may be an effort to achieve a new kind of connection with the universe, working within the framework that is acceptable to the Western scientific model. Perhaps SETI is an acceptable way for us to seek that reintegration, a feeling of connectedness which has been shattered by standing apart from the cosmos and examining it as something that is not alive, not intelligent, and separate from ourselves."

Cooperation or Conflict

4. Cooperation in Joint Galactic Projects.

We might eventually play a role in some grand galactic project in art, science, philosophy, or philanthropy. Such projects might aim to solve fundamental mysteries of the universe, help other civilizations develop and flourish, or spread harmonious intelligent life throughout the galaxy.

In *The Extraterrestrial Encyclopedia*, Joseph Angelo has noted that contact "might lead to the development of branches of art and science that simply cannot be undertaken by just one planetary civilization but rather require joint, multiple-civilization participation across interstellar distances. Perhaps the very survival and salvation of the human race depends on finding ourselves cast in a larger cosmic role—a role far greater in significance than any human can now imagine."

5. Long-term Negative Effects.

If we incorporate extraterrestrial knowledge and advice into our human society, we may experience severe disruption, at least for a short time. We might suffer from enormous culture shock, temporarily feel inferior, or lose confidence in our own culture. Massive and rapid change could occur in the sciences if extraterrestrial science is deeply different, in business and industry if we learn about new processes and products, in the legal system if we move toward cosmic or universal laws, and in the armed forces and their suppliers if we eliminate the threat of war. Probably all of this should be regarded as simply the major cost we have to pay for incorporating new knowledge and possibilities. But will the short-term chaos and conflict be so severe that the negative consequences continue for decades or centuries?

Will our human culture (and even our genes) be obliterated by a more advanced civilization?

Will our science or philosophy "lose its nerve" when faced with far superior knowledge, and permanently retreat into trivia or resistance rather than embracing the new?

What other sorts of negative effects might be profound and long lasting?

"What Next?"

After exploring those five sorts of impact, the seminar participants turned to the question of "What next?" in their final session together. What should humanity do *now* in order to maximize the positive long-term impact from an eventual dialogue—in order to achieve the greatest possible benefits for our culture, science, worldview, and long-term future?

For me personally, the highlight of the seminar occurred during the exploration of this topic when Keiko Tokunaga, a young Buddhist priest, brought a fresh perspective to the discussion. Emphasizing the personal level, she gently pointed out the need for all of us to become better prepared for contact with an alien intelligence. Our own personal growth could enable us to be more sensitive to the signals that we may be inadvertently sending out to extraterrestrial intelligence, for instance, and to reduce our ego and our defenses so that we become truly open to contact with something so alien—truly warm, welcoming, receptive, compassionate, and centered rather than scared or defensive or hostile.

SUCCESS IN SETI MIGHT HAVE NEGATIVE CONSEQUENCES

Ragbir Bhathal and Eric J. Chaisson

Two participants in a 1999 international seminar on potential consequences of contact with aliens believed that the impact of success in SETI might be negative. The following selection consists of their opening statements. Ragbir Bhathal, an award-winning author and astrophysicist, is director of the Australia-Singapore Centre at the University of Western Sydney. He argues that the culture shock Earth would experience from contact with an extraterrestrial civilization would be destructive, and that aliens might even help individual humans to manipulate humanity in the pursuit of alien agendas. Eric J. Chaisson is a professor of physics and astronomy who is also director of the H. Dudley Wright Center for Innovative Science Education at Tufts University. Chaisson suggests that although contact with extraterrestrials through communication alone would affect only a few humans and would have little impact, physical contact with any more advanced species would lead to domination of Earth even if the aliens were not overtly hostile.

Statement by Ragbir Bhathal

If it is assumed that the laws of physics and biology are the same here as elsewhere in the universe, then the evolution of life in all parts of the universe would have progressed from the simple to the complex. In the process Darwin's philosophy would have been uppermost. Almost everything in the universe would fall under the control of the most fit, most intelligent, and the strongest. The needs of this group would be justified on rational arguments and philosophies—*rational* being defined by the group to suit its own purposes and agendas. This has been the history of human civilizations throughout the ages. There is no *a priori* reason that ETI [extraterrestrial intelligence] civilizations will be any different. They would also want to control the resources of the universe or other galactic civilizations for their own ends. The history of Earth civilizations will be mirrored in the civilizations in other parts of the universe.

SETI literature normally ascribes attributes of goodness, humaneness, and a general willingness of ETI civilizations to assist the less advanced civilizations. From a Darwinian perspective, this will not necessarily be the case. This is very well illustrated by an analogue from planet Earth. At the end of the 18th century an advanced civilization landed in Australia and confronted the Aboriginal peoples of Australia. The advanced civilization had passed through the hunter and gatherer stage and the agricultural stage, and was, at the end of the 18th century, at the height of its technological development. It was at a stage where it could move over the entire oceanic and terrestrial space on Earth. When the advanced civilization arrived in Australia, there was a gap of over 10,000 years between the technologies of the advanced civilization and that of the Aboriginal peoples. Rather than treating the Aboriginal peoples in a civilized and humane manner, the advanced civilization took over their lands and in Tasmania the Aboriginal population was wiped out. It was one of the greatest genocides in the history of human civilization.

Will a much more advanced civilization do the same with us if and when they discover planet Earth within a thousand years from now? If a discovery and physical contact are made with ETI civilizations in the distant future, the culture shock we will experience will be extremely disruptive and continue for several centuries. Our institutions will be incapable of handling the crisis and it may be the end of human civilization, as we know it today. . . .

Let us look at another scenario. It may be the case that an advanced civilization need not actually make physical contact with us. ETI civilizations could use human proxies on Earth to do their bidding through high-technology intelligent probes and the galactic internet. Thus a powerful group of human proxies may be given the knowledge and technology by ETI for the control and manipulation of human populations for political and social agendas of the ETI civilization. Again, we have human analogues for this scenario. If this happens, human civilization will be in for a long culture shock and it may not recover from the disruption of its institutions.

Statement by Eric J. Chaisson

Every productive meeting needs an *agent provocateur*. Since I cannot be sure, looking at the list of attendees, that we have one among us, I shall assume that role until otherwise deposed.

My hypotheses are that there will likely be no positive effect from contact with ETI during the next thousand years. Yes, it would be nice to know if ETIs exist in space; the "commission" that astronomers have from the public to keep an eye on the universe demands that we strive to inventory cosmic life in all its forms, just as we do for matter and radiation. However, in the long run, electromagnetic (indirect) contact will probably have negligible effect on us, and physical (direct) contact will probably be harmful to us.

Should contact with ETI be limited to electromagnetic means, and there be little chance of ETI traveling to Earth (or us to their home) within the next millennium (owing largely to light-speed restrictions), then the impact of ETI on our civilization will be minimal, perhaps virtually zero, given the steady stream of "in-house" global problems inevitably confronting humankind while pushing out along the arrow of time. Of course, we shall study ETIs' signals, decipher their messages, perhaps even learn some things from them (since any ETI initiating contact with us will be, essentially by definition, more advanced and knowledgeable than we). Earth's academics will publish scholarly analyses of ETI data in the specialized cyberspace journals; commentators will propagate opinions among the bits and bytes of the new Net; and the media hype of each new ETI finding and its cultural vicissitudes will cause the mainstream press of the third millennium to resemble the tabloid press of the late-second millennium. But indirect contact alone will likely be of meaningful concern only to a small minority of Earth's citizens—essentially an ensemble of future people statistically indistinguishable from those currently interested in SETI. As long as contact remains solely electromagnetic, Earth-based global issues of (mostly) our own making will dominate our lives, indeed drive our future evolution during the next thousand years.

Should contact with ETI be physical, even as a mere ceremonial visitation, then the impact could be large and negative for our species. I refer to the universality of physical and chemical phenomena in the cosmos, and by extension to the subjects of biology and its allied behavioral sciences. In short, if neo-Darwinism (or some version of it) holds cosmically, meaning that competition is at least part of any complex being's methodology, then it is not inconceivable that they (who will be, again, more advanced than we are) would dominate us. Not that they would "come and eat us"—though they might; we do, in fact, consume many other, "lesser" species—and not that their alien posture toward us would be overtly hostile. Rather, dominance is likely to be the natural, indeed perhaps inevitable, stance of any advanced life form. It is just as reasonable to argue that advanced life, anywhere in the cosmos, will tend to control other life (as well as controlling matter and radiation locally) if given the opportunity and if in physical contact, as it is to suggest that positive consequences will result from our detection of and interaction with extraterrestrial intelligence.

If Aliens Are Visiting Earth, Their Motives Are Probably Not Benign

Michael D. Swords

Michael D. Swords is professor emeritus of the Environmental Institute, Western Michigan University, Kalamazoo, and former editor of the *Journal of UFO Studies*. In the following selection he states his belief that UFOs are probably of extraterrestrial origin and speculates about the possible motives of aliens who visit Earth. He sees no evidence that UFOs and alien visitors are benign, but he does not agree with the view of investigators Budd Hopkins and David Jacobs, who believe that they are producing cross-species hybrids through genetic engineering. In Swords's opinion, they are most likely meddling with Earth and its inhabitants simply as a game for their own amusement.

This article is a speculation about the meaning of the UFO phenomenon. Its value, if any, might be to stimulate discussion about the big questions in our field and perhaps clarify or put a few matters in focus. My only excuse for presenting this is that I've had a lot of years in the UFO trenches and listened to a lot of the best ideas of my fellow UFO workers. So, here are my thoughts, for what they are worth.

My discussion is based upon a few assumptions. The major one is that the best case reports are responses to and glimpses of high technology that we humans do not produce. In brief defense of this assumption, I can only offer the huge panoply of excellent cases, anchored by such reports as Boianai, Papua New Guinea ("Father Gill"), the Coyne helicopter case in Ohio, or the Nash-Fortenberry mid-air encounter. In my own family are two rather impressive silent-disk cases that would just be swallowed up by the hundreds of stunning close encounters of the first kind. The extraterrestrial hypothesis (ETH) is not the only theory that we can use for these cases, but it is the simplest, and in many ways, the least stretch of the imagination as far as expanding what we currently believe to be likely about our universe.

Some people argue that the ETH is insufficient to deal with many

Michael D. Swords, "What Does a Half Century of Intense UFO Display Mean?" *International UFO Reporter*, Fall 2001. *IUR* is a publication of the J. Allen Hynek Center for UFO Studies, Chicago, IL. Reproduced by permission of the author.

elements of UFO phenomenology. To them I say two things: 1) they are probably the ones who are lacking in imagination, if they cannot envision some of the near "magical" potentialities that the futurists and nano- and information-technologists are already talking about today; and 2) not *every* experience reported to a ufologist need be true, nor need it be related to the UFO phenomenon. If there is a scattering of reports that don't seem to fit well into the ETH, this should not be much of a surprise. Don't throw them away, but don't assume that they necessarily belong or that we have all the insight and creativity needed to explain every reported experience. Instead, let's give the ETH a chance and ride with it awhile in the context of this article's background, i.e., the 50-year display of the UFO phenomenon—not hidden but readily visible to our civilization.

Our recent discoveries of extrasolar planets have heightened the discussion of SETI, the Drake equation, and the odds of a galaxy full of various kinds of intelligent life. The discussion has led scientists to predict that most life-bearing stars would be older (some far older) than the Sun, and the odds would be that life there was advanced beyond us as well. Ufology has been saying the same thing for decades. Any beings capable of the technology that we observe would be significantly advanced (and probably vastly advanced) beyond where we are today. And this view is not only modern scientific deduction, it has always been common sense. The thought arose almost immediately with the military and intelligence people studying the early cases, and, if it weren't for the lack of imagination of their various astronomically trained consultants, who knows how long the ETH would have persisted as an open theory among those circles. There is another obvious point. Whenever we decide to call ourselves a spacefaring civilization, we will by definition be the newest and most technologically crude one doing so. *Everybody else* flying around will be smarter and have been doing it longer than us.

So, just for the sake of discussion, let's imagine that most of the very good, unexplained UFO cases are the product of ET technology, and that this technology is from a civilization that's not only smarter than us, but vastly smarter. We now face the questions that motivated this article. Why are they here? Why have they kept up this strange peek-a-boo display for half a century in a somewhat intense manner?

Extraterrestrial Motivations

We would expect that most beings do things because they have a *need*, but often also because they have a *desire*. "Need" here is meant to (roughly) indicate an urgent survival issue; "desire" indicates something one *could* do without but is nevertheless driven towards anyway. These two categories tend to fog together in a mind dominated by emotion and illogic. Whether need or desire, ET behavior would be motivated purely by self-interest.

A second class of motivations, which some philosophers will argue are really not separate (though I disagree), are motives based on altruism or genuine caring for "the other" without regard to anything one might get out of the behavior. The typical SETI enthusiast is always talking about the great-hearted ET-altruists who are just waiting their opportunity to send us their Encyclopedia Galactica of knowledge which will end resource and energy shortages, famine, cancer, death, and even war.

Using that as a rough roadmap, let's tease out some of the specifics. Since we know ourselves best, let's begin with altruistic ET motivations of what they might want to do for us and compare that to the UFO phenomenon and its time frame of 50 years of display.

We imperfect Earthlings have many needs that a beneficent savior could ameliorate. We have terrible food, water, and resource problems in many areas of the world. We have created technological systems upon which many of us are totally dependent, but which have serious, perhaps even terminal, side effects on health, ecology, and our ability to sustain these into the future. Ubiquitous communication systems spread news (accurate or not) to "have-nots" about what the "haves" are doing and, in the process, incite war and terrorism. Science is so advanced and moral values so weak that groups and individuals have all they need in terms of weapons and attitudes to pursue an agenda of terror and harm. And this is just what we've wreaked upon ourselves. Beyond this, we could really use some help with cancer, AIDS, the aging process, etc. A recent worry is the occasional wayward asteroid or comet, and even the wayward meddling ET-civilization.

ETs Are Not Helping Humankind

How does a review of the UFO phenomenon relate to these concerns? Do we have *any* valid and convincing evidence that we are being helped in any of these areas? Are the high-tech ETs who seem to be cruising about, displaying their powerful knowledge in their devices, demonstrably altruists? I see precisely zero evidence for this thesis. There have been no cures, no miracle devices, no functional "gifts" at all. Every time something of this sort arises, it eventually leads to nothing. Fairy tales persist among contactee circles and conspiracy cults, but nothing materializes . . . exactly nothing. Some abduction investigators claim that individuals have been helped. Maybe. Even if true—and it is just as conceivable that these individuals have helped *themselves* get through an intense experience or problem—the scattering of persons aided by the ETs is pretty meager when compared to the population of six billion humans. Such assistance appears to be a side effect, at best.

The only way of saving the "ETs are altruists" theory is to assume that they want to do this, but have decided that it isn't time yet. This is possible, but it's pretty thin gruel to feed on. Some say that the ETs are conditioning us for overt contact. After we are ready, they will then bring out the goodies. This is, of course, possible, particularly if we add that they want all cultures and religions to be accepting enough to have equal opportunity to share in the gifts when the contact is made. But over 55 years—since at least 1947—is an awfully patient (and inefficient) process. That is long enough that any competent ET civilization should have accomplished the necessary groundwork by now, if their plan was simply conditioning us to the idea that they are here and trustworthy gift-givers.

Could ET be altruistically protecting us from large and destructive collisions with space debris? Well, yes. But they can do that just fine "way out there" somewhere, without us knowing about it. More to the point, that activity would bear no relationship whatsoever to buzzing people in automobiles down here on Earth. So ufology offers no support for that idea, either. Could ET be protecting us from other bad or malevolent ETs? Well, yes to that question, too. But it's a useless concept in this current discussion. It just begs the question of what the other ETs are doing here then, although the answer must be nothing altruistic, or we wouldn't need saving from them. No, our UFO-driving ETs don't seem to be altruists.

Why Are They Interested in Earth?

They are here for their own interests, then. And, what could be more natural? Beings pursue their *own* agendas. But *what* about Earth, and us? Could they be interested enough in us to play peek-a-boo for 50 years?

Let's address the basic physical nature of our solar system. An advanced scientific and technological society would figure out our physics, astronomy, chemistry, and geology in a week, maybe a few hours. If they were here to explore and gain pure knowledge (the ET scholars), they could pack up and move on without us ever seeing them. And, before they even arrived, they would know that there was nothing physical or chemical here that they *needed*. It has always astonished me to listen to people mulling the possibilities that the ETs needed our uranium or water. Imagine these supertechnologists: coming all this way to get a drink. Civilizations this advanced do not need any help getting resources. Basic energy and chemicals abound all over the galaxy. We are not special in the solar system. If we are, it is because of our emergent phenomena: life, intelligence, society.

Would explorer-scholar ETs be interested in the life forms of Earth? Probably. With their previous knowledge, analytical abilities, and data-sorting and sifting capability, it would most likely take them a few weeks to figure it all out. DNA is a miracle, but it ain't *that* complicated. The understanding of how our fauna and flora function (and came to be) would rapidly fall into meaningful patterns, just as it slowly has done for us. It certainly wouldn't take 50 years.

Would explorer-scholars be interested in higher mental activities, and sociocultural structures? Very probably. They are more complex fields, harder to predict. Would it take longer for them to understand our society? I'd guess so, especially if they wanted to set up experiments to test whatever hypotheses they had. These experiments shouldn't take long if directed only to the individual mind (on an instincts, emotions, reasoning level), but could be quite lengthy if they were society-wide macroexperiments. Of all the hypotheses mentioned so far, this concept is the only one that seems to fit well with a 50-year semicovert display. It would be a thing of sufficient subtlety: a velvet-touch manipulation without direct meddling in our technological, economic, or political situations. Throw stones in their pond, and watch how far this species allows the ripples to go.

There are a couple of other characteristics of we humans that the explorer-scholars might be interested in as well. Despite our tendencies toward materialism, there are those of us who maintain an intouchness with the spiritual, and with the paranormal. This may be something that they are vitally interested in, and some aspect of it may be a feature that they cannot find in themselves. Our own difficulties in achieving these states of consciousness may require a lengthy period of study. Even then, the open display aspect of the phenomenon does not fit well with these latter interests, as it does with the societal experimentation idea.

Malevolent Extraterrestrials

Let us leave the relatively benign explorer-scholar theory behind and address hotter and nastier hypotheses. If humans can supply the solution to a need for these advanced extraterrestrials, what could it be? ETs can create all the energy and all the biological substances they require (even "genes") off the shelves of their labs. Does our system itself have any *strategic* importance? For a society that can warp in and out of Space-Time by super technology, that seems unlikely. Could they have a prophecy that somehow involves us? That's pretty species-centric to imagine that, but I suppose that it is possible that we are their equivalent of Bethlehem. But that doesn't really seem likely. If they are driven to remain here for as long as they have been observed, they *want* to, they don't *need* to.

So what about wants? We could be facing a very religious civilization (religious rather than spiritual—one bound by inflexible duties rather than compassion and empathy). And it could be their sacred trust to convert the Earth to their view. But they know how powerful our own religions and spiritualities are, and they realize that it will take a long and clever conditioning before they can become completely overt and begin the conversion in earnest. Such a hypothesis could account for an extremely subtle and patient phenomenological display. Whether we would get Saganesque goodies [benefits of the kind suggested by astronomer Carl Sagan] along with the sermons, who knows? It could be the galactic version of going to the Gospel Mission soup kitchen. Before dispensing with this idea too quickly, we should remember that very few things will motivate Earthlings to extreme efforts, and religious fervor is one of them. The fools of the Hale-Bopp fiasco [the death of the Heaven's Gate cultists, whose suicide was influenced by their belief in a UFO following the Hale-Bopp comet] would be a nearly unrelated and unfortunate side effect to this subtle game, but one wonders whether the believers in the John Mack school of spiritual abductions would see no seeds planted for this agenda.

There are much nastier possibilities to contemplate. Having mentioned John Mack, veteran ufologists will immediately think of his opposite school: the Hopkins-Jacobs school of cold, uncaring genetic hybridizers. Well, cold and uncaring I can easily credit. And my views on the *in*credibility of real cross-species hybridization are well known to Budd [Hopkins] and Dave [Jacobs]. Since they are friends whom I like a great deal, I'll say no more on that subject here. Plus, I can see what is for me a much simpler hypothesis to account for all the terrorizing, messing-with-one's-mind-and-emotions that is said to go on in a classic CE-4 [close encounter of the fourth kind]. We are cannon fodder for their entertainment.

Games Aliens Might Play

Suppose one was a member of a truly high-tech civilization. We could not only shoot around the galaxy in disks, but also cure diseases, prevent aging, and avoid most accidents. We'd be nearly immortal. And there might not be much work to do, either. We'd have a leisure-time paradise. But would it be that? Forever is a really long time. What, after the first couple hundred years, would be have to look forward to? Maybe the cleverer of us would find some bottomless mystery to devote our hours and days to, but what of the rest? What do you do when you've seen and experienced it all? Drugs? Sex? Probably. But even then, what, ultimately, is new? A very advanced, very long-lived species might have a gigantic need for novelty—nothing profound, just as entertainment.

Suppose that you could meddle, subtly, with an entire world. On the macroscale, you could play that world like a vast, concrete, unpredictable game. Show them a little something here, what will they do? Mess with some military installations there, then what? Maybe even fake a disk crash for them. This theory sounds a bit like the anthropological-scholars running experiments, but it is sufficiently different. Here the audience is not scholars (who might quit when they've gotten enough data), but the alien equivalent of fantasy football–league players who may want to go on, and even escalate their meddling, forever. As far as evidence goes, whether there is truth to the theory or not, the 50-year peek-a-boo display certainly has subtly messed with our minds about what's true about the world.

And suppose that for some ETs these macrosocietal games weren't down-and-dirty enough. How about using your nanotechnology to create implant linkages between yourself and an Earthling, and then titillating or terrorizing the hell out of that person, virtually experiencing the rush of their emotions? Of course, no one wants to believe that. No one wants to feel like they're being used, especially with no say in the matter. But it would explain much of what is reported in abductions. And, possibly, it would keep the bored, uncaring, nastier element of the ET society entertained. As long as it worked, meeting their needs, why ever quit? Why not thousands of psychological terrorist acts, if they had a powerful desire and the ability and the immorality to pursue it?

No Evidence That ETs Are Benign

Many in our field have stated their belief (wish, I think) that the ETs are good guys. I see no evidence of it. I feel that the best we can hope for is that they have relatively benign and temporary interests in us, and that they will go away without doing any permanent damage.

You can invent more theories than I've discussed here. All of the above ideas refer to very advanced ETs, and are tested against the need to explain the 50-year dance we've been seeing. In my view, the theories that survive the test best are the macroscopic societal-manipulation ones (for religious conversion, or anthropological research, or entertainment on a grand scale), and the ultranasty concept that might be called emotional parasitism. All these ideas originate from considering what the ETs want for themselves. The only altruistic theory that seems plausible is the macrosocietal manipulation so that all Earthlings will be conditioned to equally share in whatever goodies the ETs bring. Since this latter seems much more concrete in its goal, i.e., dumping real undeniable stuff on us, it seems to need less subtlety to set up, and perhaps not such a long dance of sightings. The others appear to require much more covert action, as we have experienced.

I realize that speculations are not great contributions to ufological research. Forgive me. I'm doing my part to entertain the aliens. Writing articles such as this is much more pleasant than being victimized by Budd and Dave's "mind scanners."

THE DISCOVERY OF EXTRATERRESTRIAL LIFE WOULD IMPACT WORLD RELIGIONS

Paul Davies

Paul Davies, an internationally acclaimed physicist and cosmologist, is a professor of natural philosophy at the Australian Centre for Astrobiology, located at Macquarie University in Sydney, Australia. He is the author of twenty-five science books and has won several prestigious awards in the fields of science and religion. In the following article, Davies deals with the questions that the discovery of extraterrestrial life would pose for established religions. Davies argues that among Christians, there is diversity of opinion about how disruptive this discovery would be to religious beliefs (which has been the case ever since the seventeenth century). To adherents of some other major world religions—Muslims, Buddhists, and Hindus for example—such a discovery would not seem spiritually threatening, Davies maintains. He even explains that there are now minority religions specifically focused on UFOs. Would advanced alien beings share the spiritual dimension of human nature? Davies states that many people think so, and some think that whether or not aliens do, knowledge that life exists beyond Earth would enhance new human conceptions of God.

The recent discovery of abundant water on Mars, albeit in the form of permafrost, has raised hopes for finding traces of life there. The Red Planet has long been a favorite location for those speculating about extraterrestrial life, especially since the 1890s, when [science fiction author] H.G. Wells wrote *The War of the Worlds* and the American astronomer Percival Lowell claimed that he could see artificial canals etched into the planet's parched surface. Today, of course, scientists expect to find no more than simple bacteria dwelling deep underground, if even that. Still, the discovery of just a single bacterium somewhere beyond Earth would force us to revise our understanding of who we are and where we fit into the cosmic scheme of things, throwing us into a deep spiritual identity crisis that would be every bit as dramatic as the one Copernicus brought about in the early 1500s, when he asserted that Earth was not at the center of the universe.

Whether or not we are alone is one of the great existential questions that confront us today. Probably because of the high emotional stakes, the search for life beyond Earth is deeply fascinating to the public. Opinion polls and Web-site hits indicate strong support for and interest in space missions that are linked even obliquely to this search. Perceiving the public's interest, NASA has reconfigured its research strategy and founded the NASA Astrobiology Institute, dedicated to the study of life in the cosmos. . . .

The prospects for finding living organisms on Mars remain slim, of course, but even traces of past life would represent a discovery of unprecedented scientific value. Before any sweeping philosophical or theological conclusions could be drawn, however, it would be necessary to determine whether this life was the product of a second genesis—that is, whether its origin was independent of life on Earth. Earth and Mars are known to trade material in the form of rocks blasted from the planets' surfaces by the violent impacts of asteroids and comets. Microbes could have hitched a ride on this detritus, raising the possibility that life started on Earth and was transferred to Mars, or vice versa. If traces of past life were discovered on Mars but found to be identical to some form of terrestrial life, transportation by ejected rocks would be the most plausible explanation, and we would still lack evidence that life had started from scratch in two separate locations.

The significance of this point is crucial. In his theory of evolution Charles Darwin provided a persuasive account of how life evolved over billions of years, but he pointedly omitted any explanation of how life got started in the first place. "One might as well think of origin of matter," he wrote in a letter to a friend. A century and a half later, scientists still have little understanding of how the first living thing came to be.

Is Life a Freak Accident?

Some scientists believe that life on Earth is a freak accident of chemistry, and as such must be unique. Because even the simplest known microbe is breathtakingly complex, they argue, the chances that one formed by blind molecular shuffling are infinitesimal; the probability that the process would occur twice, in separate locations, is virtually negligible. The French biochemist and Nobel laureate Jacques Monod was a firm believer in this view. "Man at last knows he is alone in the unfeeling immensity of the universe, out of which he has emerged only by chance," he wrote in 1971. He used this bleak assessment as a springboard to argue for atheism and the absurdity and pointlessness of existence. As Monod saw it, we are merely chemical extras in a majestic but impersonal cosmic drama—an irrelevant, unintended sideshow.

But suppose that's not what happened. Many scientists believe that life is not a freakish phenomenon (the odds of life's starting by chance, the British cosmologist Fred Hoyle once suggested, are comparable to the odds of a whirlwind's blowing through a junkyard and assembling a functioning Boeing 747) but instead is written into the laws of nature. "The universe must in some sense have known we were coming," the physicist Freeman Dyson famously observed. No one can say precisely in what sense the universe might be pregnant with life, or how the general expectancy Dyson spoke of might translate into specific physical processes at the molecular level. Perhaps matter and energy always get fast-tracked along the road to life by what's often called "self-organization." Or perhaps the power of Darwinian evolution is somehow harnessed at a pre-biotic molecular stage. Or maybe some efficient and as yet unidentified physical process (quantum mechanics?) sets the gears in motion, with organic life as we know it taking over the essential machinery at a later stage. Under any of these scenarios life becomes a fundamental rather than an incidental product of nature. In 1994, reflecting on this same point, another Nobel laureate, the Belgian biochemist Christian de Duve, wrote, "I view this universe not as a 'cosmic joke,' but as a meaningful entity—made in such a way as to generate life and mind, bound to give birth to thinking beings able to discern truth, apprehend beauty, feel love, yearn after goodness, define evil, experience mystery."

Absent from these accounts is any mention of miracles. Ascribing the origin of life to a divine miracle not only is anathema to scientists but also is theologically suspect. The term "God of the gaps" was coined to deride the notion that God can be invoked as an explanation whenever scientists have gaps in their understanding. The trouble with invoking God in this way is that as science advances, the gaps close, and God gets progressively squeezed out of the story of nature. Theologians long ago accepted that they would forever be fighting a rearguard battle if they tried to challenge science on its own ground. Using the formation of life to prove the existence of God is a tactic that risks instant demolition should someone succeed in making life in a test tube. And the idea that God acts in fits and starts, moving atoms around on odd occasions in competition with natural forces, is a decidedly uninspiring image of the Grand Architect.

Chance or Certitude

The theological battle line in relation to the formation of life is not, therefore, between the natural and the miraculous but between sheer chance and lawlike certitude. Atheists tend to take the first side, and theists line up behind the second; but these divisions are general and by no means absolute. It's perfectly possible to be an atheist and believe that life is built ingeniously into the nature of the universe. It's also possible to be a theist and suppose that God engineered just one planet with life, with or without the help of miracles.

Though the discovery of microbes on Mars or elsewhere would ignite a passionate theological debate, the truly difficult issues surround the prospect of advanced alien beings in possession of intelligence and technology. Most scientists don't think that such beings exist, but for forty years a dedicated band of astronomers has been sweeping the skies with radio telescopes in hopes of finding a message from a civilization elsewhere in the galaxy. Their project is known as SETI (Search for Extraterrestrial Intelligence).

Because our solar system is relatively young compared with the universe overall, any alien civilization the SETI researchers might discover is likely to be much older, and presumably wiser, than ours. Indeed, it might have achieved our level of science and technology millions or even billions of years ago. Just contemplating the possibility of such advanced extraterrestrials appears to raise additional uncomfortable questions for religion.

The world's main faiths were all founded in the prescientific era, when Earth was widely believed to be at the center of the universe and humankind at the pinnacle of creation. As scientific discoveries have piled up over the past 500 years, our status has been incrementally diminished. First Earth was shown to be just one planet of several orbiting the Sun. Then the solar system itself was relegated to the outer suburbs of the galaxy, and the Sun classified as an insignificant dwarf star among billions. The theory of evolution proposed that human beings occupied just a small branch on a complex evolutionary tree. This pattern continued into the twentieth century, when the supremacy of our much vaunted intelligence came under threat. Computers began to outsmart us. Now genetic engineering has raised the specter of designer babies with superintellects that leave ours far behind. And we must consider the uncomfortable possibility that in astrobiological terms, God's children may be galactic also-rans.

The Diversity of Views Within Christianity

Theologians are used to putting a brave face on such developments. Over the centuries the Christian church, for example, has time and again been forced to accommodate new scientific facts that challenge existing doctrine. But these accommodations have usually been made reluctantly and very belatedly. . . . If SETI succeeds, theologians will not have the luxury of decades of careful deliberation to assess the significance of the discovery. The impact will be instant.

The discovery of alien superbeings might not be so corrosive to religion if human beings could still claim special spiritual status. After all, religion is concerned primarily with people's relationship to God, rather than with their biological or intellectual qualities. It is possible to imagine alien beings who are smarter and wiser than we are but who are spiritually inferior, or just plain evil. However, it is more likely that any civilization that had surpassed us scientifically would have improved on our level of moral development, too. One may even speculate that an advanced alien society would sooner or later find some way to genetically eliminate evil behavior, resulting in a race of saintly beings.

Suppose, then, that E.T. is far ahead of us not only scientifically and technologically but spiritually, too. Where does that leave mankind's presumed special relationship with God? . . . Can we contemplate a universe that contains perhaps a trillion worlds of saintly beings, but in which the only beings eligible for salvation inhabit a planet where murder, rape, and other evils remain rife? . . . [Theologian Ted] Peters believes that Christianity is robust enough and flexible enough to accommodate the discovery of extraterrestrial intelligence, or ETI. One theologian who is emphatically not afraid of that challenge is Robert Russell, also of the Center for Theology and the Natural Sciences. "As we await 'first contact,'" he has written, "pursuing these kinds of questions and reflections will be immensely valuable."

Clearly, there is considerable diversity—one might even say muddle—on this topic in theological circles. Ernan McMullin, a professor emeritus of philosophy at Notre Dame University, affirms that the central difficulty stems from Christianity's roots in a pre-scientific cosmology. . . . Pointing out that concepts such as original sin, incarnation, and salvation are open to a variety of interpretations, McMullin concludes that there is also widespread divergence among Christians on the correct response to the ETI challenge. On the matter of multiple incarnations he writes, "Their answers could range . . . from 'yes, certainly' to 'certainly not.' My own preference would be a cautious 'maybe?'"

Even for those Christians who dismiss the idea of multiple incarnations there is an interesting fallback position: perhaps the course of evolution has an element of directionality, with humanlike beings the inevitable end product. Even if *Homo sapiens* as such may not be the unique focus of God's attention, the broader class of all humanlike beings in the universe might be. This is the basic idea espoused by the philosopher Michael Ruse, an ardent Darwinian and an agnostic sympathetic to Christianity. He sees the incremental progress of natural evolution as God's chosen mode of creation, and the history of life as a ladder that leads inexorably from microbes to man.

Are Humans the Goal of Evolution?

Most biologists regard a "progressive evolution," with human beings its implied preordained goal, as preposterous. Stephen Jay Gould once described the very notion as "noxious." After all, the essence of Darwinism is that nature is blind. It cannot look ahead. Random chance is the driving force of evolution, and randomness by definition has no directionality. Gould insisted that if the evolutionary tape were replayed, the result would be very different from what we now observe. Probably life would never get beyond microbes next time around.

But some respected biologists disagree sharply with Gould on this point. Christian de Duve does not deny that the fine details of evolutionary history depend on happenstance, but he believes that the broad thrust of evolutionary change is somehow innately predetermined—that plants and animals were almost destined to emerge amid a general advance in complexity. Another Darwinian biologist, Simon Conway Morris, of Cambridge University, makes his own case for a "ladder of progress," invoking the phenomenon of convergent evolution—the tendency of similar-looking organisms to evolve independently in similar ecological niches. For example, the Tasmanian tiger (now extinct) played the role of the big cat in Australia even though, as a marsupial, it was genetically far removed from placental mammals. Like Ruse, Conway Morris maintains that the "humanlike niche" is likely to be filled on other planets that have advanced life. He even goes so far as to argue that extraterrestrials would have a humanoid form. It is not a great leap from this conclusion to the belief that extraterrestrials would sin, have consciences, struggle with ethical questions, and fear death.

Some Religions Are Prepared for Discovery of ETI

The theological difficulties posed by the possibility of advanced alien beings are less acute for Judaism and Islam. Muslims, at least, are prepared for ETI: the Koran states explicitly. "And among His Signs is the creation of the heavens and the earth, and the living creatures that He has scattered through them." Nevertheless, both religions stress the specialness of human beings—and, indeed, of specific, well-defined groups who have been received into the faith. Could an alien become a Jew or a Muslim? Does the concept even make sense? Among the major religious communities, Buddhists and Hindus would seem to be the least threatened by the prospect of advanced aliens, owing to their pluralistic concept of God and their traditionally much grander vision of the cosmos.

Among the world's minority religions, some would positively welcome the discovery of intelligent aliens. The Raëlians, a Canada-based cult recently propelled to fame by its claim to have cloned a human being, believe that the cult's leader, Raël, a French former journalist originally named Claude Vorilhon, received revelations from aliens who briefly transported him inside a flying saucer in 1973. Other fringe religious organizations with an extraterrestrial message include the ill-fated Heaven's Gate cult and many UFO groups. Their adherents share a belief that aliens are located further up not only the evolutionary ladder but also the spiritual ladder, and can therefore help us draw closer to

God and salvation. It is easy to dismiss such beliefs as insignificant to serious theological debate, but if evidence for alien beings were suddenly to appear, these cults might achieve overnight prominence while established religions floundered in doctrinal bewilderment.

Ironically, SETI is often accused of being a quasi-religious quest. But Jill Tarter, the director of the SETI Institute's Center for SETI Research, in Mountain View, California, has no truck with religion and is contemptuous of the theological gymnastics with which religious scholars accommodate the possibility of extraterrestrials. "God is our own invention," she has written. "If we're going to survive or turn into a long-lived technological civilization, organized religion needs to be outgrown. If we get a message [from an alien civilization] and it's secular in nature, I think that says that they have no organized religion—that they've outgrown it." Tarter's dismissal is rather naive, however. Though many religious movements have come and gone throughout history, some sort of spirituality seems to be part of human nature. Even atheistic scientists profess to experience what Albert Einstein called a "cosmic religious feeling" when contemplating the awesome majesty of the universe.

Would advanced alien beings share this spiritual dimension, even though they might long ago have "outgrown" established religion? Steven Dick, a science historian at the U.S. Naval Observatory, believes they would. Dick is an expert on the history of speculation about extraterrestrial life, and he suggests that mankind's spirituality would be greatly expanded and enriched by contact with an alien civilization. However, he envisages that our present concept of God would probably require a wholesale transformation. Dick has outlined what he calls a new "cosmotheology," in which human spirituality is placed in a full cosmological and astrobiological context. "As we learn more about our place in the universe," he has written, "and as we physically move away from our home planet, our cosmic consciousness will only increase." Dick proposes abandoning the transcendent God of monotheistic religion in favor of what he calls a "natural God"—a superbeing located within the universe and within nature. "With due respect for present religious traditions whose history stretches back nearly four millennia," he suggests, "the natural God of cosmic evolution and the biological universe, not the supernatural God of the ancient Near East, may be the God of the next millennium.". . .

A Resurgence of the Design Argument

Though in some ways the prospect of discovering extraterrestrial life undermines established religions, it is not all bad news for them. Astrobiology has also led to a surprising resurgence of the so-called "design argument" for the existence of God. The original design argument, as articulated by William Paley in the eighteenth century, was that living organisms' intricate adaptation to their environments pointed to the providential hand of a benign Creator. Darwin demolished the argument by showing how evolution driven by random mutation and natural selection could mimic design. Now a revamped design argument has emerged that fully embraces the Darwinian account of evolution and focuses instead on the origin of life. (I must stress that I am not referring here to what has recently become known as the Intelligent Design movement, which relies on an element of the miraculous.) If life is found to be widespread in the universe, the new design argument goes, then it must emerge rather easily from nonliving chemical mixtures, and thus the laws of nature must be cunningly contrived to unleash this remarkable and very special state of matter, which itself is a conduit to an even more remarkable and special state: mind. This sort of exquisite bio-friendliness would represent an extraordinary and unexpected bonus among nature's inventory of principles—one that could be interpreted by those of a religious persuasion as evidence of God's ingenuity and foresight. In this version of cosmic design, God acts not by direct intervention but by creating appropriate natural laws that guarantee the emergence of life and mind in cosmic abundance. The universe, in other words, is one in which there are no miracles except the miracle of nature itself.

The E.T. debate has only just begun, but a useful starting point is simply to acknowledge that the discovery of extraterrestrial life would not have to be theologically devastating. The revamped design argument offers a vision of nature distinctly inspiring to the spiritually inclined—certainly more so than that of a cosmos sterile everywhere but on a single planet. History is instructive in this regard. Four hundred years ago Giordano Bruno was burned at the stake by the Church in Rome for, among other things, espousing the notion of a plurality of inhabited worlds. To those whose theological outlook depended on a conception of Earth and its life forms as a singular miracle, the very notion of extraterrestrial life proved deeply threatening. But today the possibility of extraterrestrial life is anything but spiritually threatening. The more one accepts the formation of life as a natural process (that is, the more deeply embedded one believes it is in the overall cosmic scheme), the more ingenious and contrived (dare one say "designed"?) the universe appears to be.

THE EXTRATERRESTRIAL LIFE DEBATE AFFECTS HUMANITY'S WORLD VIEW

Steven J. Dick

Steven J. Dick is an astronomer and historian of science at the U.S. Naval Observatory in Washington, D.C. He is the author of many books on past and present views of extraterrestrial life. The following selection is from a May 2000 lecture he gave at the Dibner Library of the Smithsonian Institution. In it, he discusses the importance of ideas about extraterrestrial life to society's world view, a term he defines earlier in the lecture as "how we see the world from a variety of perspectives, carrying with it an implication that world views have impact on our daily lives." He refers to the two main world views of the seventeenth century—the geocentric view of Earth as the center of the universe versus the heliocentric view, which put the sun in the center—and points out that today there are again two mutually exclusive world views. He describes them as the "physical universe" view that "cosmic evolution commonly ends in planets, stars, and galaxies" and the "biological universe" view that "it commonly ends in life, mind, and intelligence." And, he says, "The fact of life on Earth proves neither world view because it is a sample of one, and no law, theory, or world view can be proven from a sample of one." He then goes on to explain why the search for extraterrestrial life, regardless of its outcome, affects human civilization.

Just as the two chief world systems of the 17th century had profound implications for humanity, so too will our modern two chief world systems. And the implications of the two world views are very different. If we live in a physical universe where the ultimate product of cosmic evolution is planets, stars, and galaxies, it may be human destiny to populate the universe rather than to interact with extraterrestrials. Humanity would eventually *become* the extraterrestrials. It would be the universe of [science fiction author] Isaac Asimov's *Foundation* series rather than the universe of [author] Arthur C. Clarke's

Steven J. Dick, *Dibner Library Lecture*. Washington, DC: Smithsonian Institution Libraries, 2000. Copyright © 2000 by Steven J. Dick. Reproduced by permission.

Childhood's End and *2001: A Space Odyssey.*

A biological universe would be considerably more interesting, and perhaps this is one of the psychological reasons that many favor it. In discussing its implications we must . . . distinguish the weak [no complex ET life] from the strong [ET intelligence] version. By curious Congressional mandate, NASA's astrobiology program concentrates only on microbial life. Perhaps we can all agree that the discovery of microbes will have less effect than the discovery of intelligence. Barring an *Andromeda Strain* scenario, in the weak biological universe there will be no *Close Encounters of the Third Kind*, no *Independence Day*, no *ET*, and no *Contact*. Any *Star Wars* will be limited to humanity's descendants. One might argue that, because even the discovery of possible Martian fossils raised a great debate at all levels of society worldwide, so should the discovery of microbial life. But I believe that the discovery of fossils or microbes derives much of its impact from the fact that it is the first step on the road to intelligence, though longer than most people think. It would have great scientific interest, but might not necessitate the realignment of theologies and world philosophies. Nonetheless, a microbial universe has its own set of consequences; the three fundamental questions in NASA's astrobiology program (the origin and evolution of life, the existence of extraterrestrial life, and the future of life on Earth and beyond) have important cultural implications that social scientists should address.

Implications of Extraterrestrial Intelligence

The problem of the implications of the strong biological universe has been considered in some detail, notably by a NASA team in the early 1990s, and can be subjected to systematic inquiry. One approach to the implications of extraterrestrial intelligence has been general historical analogies, especially physical culture contacts on Earth, which usually end in disaster. But many consider physical culture contact unlikely (at least in the form of UFOs if not probes or microprobes), and in any case it is only one scenario among many that might be considered. Perhaps more suitable is the analogy of the transmission of knowledge from Greece to the Latin West via the Arabs. Such encounters—which historian Arnold Toynbee called "encounters between civilizations in time"—resulted in a renaissance of learning in Europe in the twelfth century, and so offer quite a different scenario than physical culture contact.

Psychologist Albert Harrison has pioneered another approach to extraterrestrial contact by applying living systems theory. This also is a kind of analog approach, relying on a systems theory in which what we know about organisms, societies and supranational systems on Earth is used to discuss the outer space analogs of aliens, alien civilizations and the galactic club. It offers the promise of bringing the social sciences into SETI in a substantive way.

Considering the biological universe as a world view . . . also offers a variety of advantages to the study of implications of contact with extraterrestrials. First, comparing like entities we can analyze the reception of past world views and ask how this might apply to the reception of the biological universe. One must always use analogs cautiously, but they are a starting point, and I have argued elsewhere that all world views undergo similar stages, ranging from their first motivation through elaboration, opposition, exploration of implications, and general acceptance or rejection. Just as the Copernican Revolution had its Galileo, Kepler and Newton, as well as its detractors, so will the biological universe. Whereas the heliocentric theory took some 150 years for widespread acceptance after Copernicus's arguments were presented, paradoxically we have the curious situation today of widespread acceptance of the biological universe *before* any solid evidence has been presented. In this regard, the exploration of implications is certainly an important stage in the life of any world view. To take only one, a primary lesson of past world views is that they harbor uncharted theological implications. The course of theological controversies for the Copernican theory and for Darwinian evolution, for example, form a rich literature in the history of science. They have a history already in the context of the extraterrestrial life debate, and the possibility of a "Cosmotheology" is receiving increasingly serious attention from scholars.

The Biological Universe in Popular Culture

A second advantage of the biological universe as world view is that elements of the debate make more sense when seen in the context of exploration of implications. I would suggest that UFOs and science fiction are two ways of working out the biological universe world view in popular culture. Although I do not see any evidence in favor of the extraterrestrial hypothesis of UFOs, the idea has undeniably had a significant impact on popular culture. A recent *Life* magazine cover story on "UFOs: Why Do We Believe?" included a poll showing that 54% of Americans believe extraterrestrial intelligence exists, 30% believe the aliens have visited Earth, and 43% believe UFOs are real, and not imaginary. One per cent (2.5 million people!) claim to have encountered an alien, but only one in five would board an alien spacecraft if invited. As for science fiction, a full range of scenarios has been explored with greater or lesser degrees of intelligence and foresight. H.G. Wells's *The War of the Worlds* (1898) expressed one stunning possible outcome of this world view. The works of Olaf Stapledon and Arthur C. Clarke, including *Star Maker* (1937), *Last and First Men* (1930), *Childhood's End* (1953), and *2001: A Space Odyssey* (1968) play out the opposite outcome. The Polish science fiction author Stanislaw Lem represents yet a third choice: in *Solaris* (1961) and *His Master's Voice* (1968) he argues that we may be unable to comprehend, much less communicate, with extraterrestrials. By the late twentieth century these themes had been elaborated in ever more subtle (and sometimes not so subtle) form. Maria Doria Russell's *The Sparrow* (1996) and *Children of God* (1998) raise powerful theological questions in an extraterrestrial context.

I am sympathetic with Lem's view that extraterrestrial communication may be much more challenging than we think. Needless to say, this has important consequences for SETI searches. In the final analysis, the problem reduces to a question of extraterrestrial epistemology, or ways of knowing. There are 3 cases in comparative terrestrial-extraterrestrial epistemology: no overlap, partial overlap, and complete overlap between human and non-human knowledge. SETI researchers usually assume complete overlap when they search for artificial transmissions. But with no overlap between human and alien minds, there would be no communication; with partial overlap the form of communication might be very different, perhaps mediated by other civilizations. Far from being an intractable problem, extraterrestrial epistemology should receive more attention in the future.

The Outcome of the Debate Will Have Impact

In closing, I must say that I am among those who believe that there is such a thing as progress in science and such things as facts in the world; either we live in a physical universe or a biological universe, either there are extraterrestrials, or there are not, and one day we will know. The whole idea of socially constructed science in a strong sense of allowing no objective knowledge seems to me to be extremely unlikely in a purely terrestrial context. There are no Chinese laws of gravity, no Islamic laws of thermodynamics, no Egyptian theory of relativity. Only one law "works" in nature, and it is to the credit of all humanity when it is discovered. The universe began in only one way, and we either have knowledge of it now, or will in the future. But when applied to extraterrestrial knowledge, social constructionism in an interspecies sense raises a more profound question: as data is filtered through many sensory systems, will alien knowledge be the same as human knowledge? Do [classics such as John] Locke's *Essay on Human Understanding*, [David] Hume's *Treatise on Human Nature*, and [Immanuel] Kant's *Critique of Pure Reason* apply to extraterrestrials? If not, in the end there may be many world systems, as many as there are cognitive systems among extraterrestrials, and some day we may have an *Essay on Non-Human Understanding*. On the question of objective knowledge, perhaps the social constructionists were ahead of their time; a century or millennium from now, perhaps our descendants will be discussing "extraterrestrial constructionism!"

In many ways a strong biological universe is more interesting. We would not be able to contemplate extraterrestrial epistemology in a universe full of bacteria. Others might be fearful that extraterrestrials would upset their current world view; they have no need of that hypothesis. Neither did religions have a need for Copernicanism, but they eventually had to adjust, though not without . . . a long and fruitless battle between science and religion. In the end, interest, need, and desire may well serve religion, but they are no criteria of truth. And although the truth about Galileo's two chief world systems is now known, the truth of the two modern world systems remains a mystery. This is precisely my point: that we teeter on the brink of a new world view that may change everything in its strong version, and a great deal even in its weak version. Even the disproof of the biological universe may have its effect.

As we stand on the threshold of a new millennium, we may conjecture that 1,000 years from now we will have had our answer to this age-old question. Humanity 3000 will know whether or not it is alone in the universe, at least within our galaxy. Olaf Stapledon's vision of "Interplanetary Humanity" fifty years ago will be extended to "Interstellar Humanity," in which our philosophy, religion, and science are much more attuned to the cosmos. By then we will know if we live in a physical or a biological universe, and we may even have traveled to the nearest stars.

I do not prejudge the outcome of the biological universe debate. But I do claim that the outcome of that debate will affect our daily lives. Extraterrestrial life is humanity's great secular meditation on the Other. It is a search for the universal laws of biology as opposed to the elaborate natural history of life on Earth that we now possess. It is becoming a new window on traditional theological concerns, as scholars broach the subject of "Cosmotheology." And, if the biological universe is proven true in the strong sense I have defined here, it has the potential to become much more than that: the universal system of thought of which our science, our art, religion, philosophy and history—in short, our knowledge and belief—are but specific instances of the manifestations of intelligence in the universe.

In short, the biological universe will affect our world view at many levels, no less than the geocentric cosmos did for Dante's contemporaries, and the heliocentric cosmos did for Galileo's, even though the full scope of the Copernican revolution was unfulfilled then, and remains so today.

ORGANIZATIONS TO CONTACT

Center for the Study of Extraterrestrial Intelligence (CSETI)
PO Box 4556, Largo, MD 20775
(888) 382-7384
e-mail: coordinator@cseti.org • Web site: www.cseti.org

CSETI is a nonprofit educational organization that aims to cultivate bilateral ETI-human contact and relations that will serve peaceful, cooperative goals. It believes ETs are currently visiting Earth and attempts to initiate communication with UFOs. It publishes books and videos.

Center for UFO Studies (CUFOS)
2457 W. Peterson Ave., Chicago, IL 60659
(773) 271-3611
e-mail: infocenter@cufos.org • Web site: www.cufos.org

CUFOS is a nonprofit scientific organization dedicated to the continuing examination and analysis of the UFO phenomenon. It promotes serious scientific interest in UFOs and serves as an archive for related reports, documents, and publications. It publishes the quarterly *Journal of UFO Studies* and the *International UFO Reporter*.

Committee for the Scientific Investigation of Claims of the Paranormal (CSICOP)
PO Box 703, Amherst, NY 14226
(716) 636-1425
e-mail: info@csicop.org • Web site: www.csicop.org

CSICOP encourages the critical investigation of paranormal and fringe-science claims from a scientific point of view and disseminates factual information about the results of such inquiries to the scientific community and the public. It deals mainly with topics unrelated to extraterrestrial life, but its site has some articles discussing UFOs from a skeptical viewpoint. It publishes the bimonthly magazine *Skeptical Inquirer*.

International Center for Abduction Research (ICAR)
12 W. Willow Grove Ave., #191, Philadelphia, PA 19118
e-mail: djacobs@ufoabduction.com • Web site: www.ufoabduction.com

ICAR was established by history professor and abduction researcher David M. Jacobs to disseminate trustworthy information about abductions to the public and to therapists who are interested in working with abductees. Dr. Jacobs believes that UFOs are a threat to humankind. He is the author of several books and publishes detailed articles at the ICAR Web site.

Intruders Foundation
PO Box 30233, New York, NY 10011
(212) 645-5278 • fax: (212) 352-1778
e-mail: ifcentral@aol.com • Web site: www.intrudersfoundation.org

The Intruders Foundation is a nonprofit organization established by ufologist Budd Hopkins to provide sympathetic help and support to those who have experienced alien abductions. It also investigates and researches the abduction phenomenon. Among its publications are the quarterly *IF Newsletter*, occasional special reports, and audio tapes.

John E. Mack Institute (JEMI)

PO Box 398080, Cambridge, MA 02139
(617) 497-2667
e-mail: info@johnemackinstitute.org • Web site: www.johnemackinstitute.org

JEMI is a nonprofit organization of scholars that grew out of Harvard psychiatrist John E. Mack's work with people who experienced alien abductions. Dr. Mack believed that such experiences are often positive. Although JEMI's activities are now focused mainly on subjects unrelated to extraterrestrial life, material about UFO abductions can be found at www.johnemackinstitute.org/projects/project.asp?id=14, which is not linked from the home page.

Mutual UFO Network (MUFON)

PO Box 369, Morrison, CO 80465-0369
(303) 932-7709 • fax: (303) 932-9279
e-mail: HQ@mufon.com • Web site: www.mufon.com

MUFON is the world's largest civilian UFO research organization, dedicated to the scientific study of UFOs for the benefit of humanity. Its members include well-known ufologists and abductees, as well as physicians, psychiatrists, psychologists, astronomers, theologians, engineers, and other scientific professionals. It investigates UFO sightings and collects the data in the MUFON database for use by researchers, in addition to promoting research on the nature of UFOs and educating the public about the phenomenon. It publishes the *MUFON UFO Journal* and *Symposium Proceedings*, which contains reports on its conferences.

NASA Astrobiology Institute

NASA Ames Research Center, Moffett Field, CA 94035-1000
(650) 604-0809 • fax: (650) 604-4251
e-mail: astrobio@www-space.arc.nasa.gov
Web site: http://nai.arc.nasa.gov

The NASA Astrobiology Institute carries out collaborative research and education in astrobiology. It publishes extensive material for scientists, teachers, students, and the public. NASA's online *Astrobiology Magazine* (www.astrobio.net) is updated daily and maintains ongoing archives.

National UFO Reporting Center

PO Box 45623, University Station, Seattle, WA 98145
(206) 722-3000
e-mail: director@ufocenter.com • Web site: www.ufocenter.com

This center serves as a headquarters for reporting possible UFO sightings. Such reports are recorded and disseminated for objective research and information purposes. The center maintains an online database of all UFO reports.

Planetary Society

65 North Catalina Ave., Pasadena, CA 91106-2301
(626) 793-5100 • fax: (626) 793-5528
e-mail: tps@planetary.org • Web site: http://planetary.org

The Planetary Society is the largest nonprofit, nongovernmental, space advocacy group on Earth, with one hundred thousand members in more than 140 countries. It is one of the very few organizations in the world that funds the search for extraterrestrial signals from other civilizations in the universe. Many detailed articles about SETI can be found at its Web site, and it publishes the bimonthly magazine *Planetary Report*.

SETI@home

Space Sciences Laboratory, University of California at Berkeley, Berkeley, CA 94720-7450
Web site: http://setiweb.ssl.berkeley.edu

SETI@home is a scientific experiment that uses Internet-connected computers in the Search for Extraterrestrial Intelligence (SETI). Anyone with a computer can participate by running a free program that downloads and analyzes radio telescope data. Detailed information is available at the Web site.

SETI Institute

515 N. Whisman Rd., Mountain View, CA 94043
(650) 961-6633 • fax: (650) 961-7099
e-mail: pio@seti.org • Web site: www.seti-inst.edu

The SETI Institute is a private, nonprofit scientific organization that aims to explore, understand, and explain the origin, nature, and prevalence of life in the universe. It conducts a comprehensive search for extraterrestrial intelligence, primarily through Project Phoenix, which uses the world's largest telescopes to search the vicinities of nearby stars for artificial signals. It publishes an e-mail newsletter and many online articles.

SETI League

433 Liberty St., PO Box 555, Little Ferry, NJ 07643
(201) 641-1770 • fax: (201) 641-1771
e-mail: info@setileague.org • Web site: www.setileague.org

The SETI League is an international network of amateur and professional scientists working together to hasten humankind's entry into the galactic community. Its members include more than one thousand amateur radio astronomers in five dozen countries on six continents. It publishes a quarterly newsletter, *SearchLites*, and a scholarly journal, *Contact in Context*.

Skeptics Society

PO Box 338, Altadena, CA 91001
(818) 794-3119 • fax: (818) 794-1301
e-mail: skepticmag@aol.com • Web site: www.skeptic.com

The Skeptics Society is a scientific and educational organization dedicated to the promotion of science and critical thinking with regard to extraordinary claims and revolutionary ideas. It investigates these areas and presents information about them that challenges uncritical belief. Although it deals primarily with subjects unrelated to extraterrestrial life, it occasionally publishes articles about UFOs in its magazine *Skeptic*.

SPACE.com

Imaginova Corporation, 470 Park Ave. S, New York, NY 10016
(212) 703-5800
Web site: www.space.com

SPACE.com is a major Internet site containing news and articles about all aspects of space exploration, including the search for life beyond Earth. It publishes only on the Web.

BIBLIOGRAPHY

Books

William A. Alschuler	*The Science of UFOs.* New York: St. Martin's, 2001.
Jeffrey Bennett, Seth Shostak, and Bruce Jakosky	*Life in the Universe.* San Francisco: Addison Wesley, 2003.
Ben Bova	*Faint Echoes, Distant Stars: The Science and Politics of Finding Life Beyond Earth.* New York: William Morrow, 2004.
William C. Burger	*Perfect Planet, Clever Species: How Unique Are We?* Amherst, NY: Prometheus, 2003.
Stuart Clark	*Life on Other Worlds and How to Find It.* New York: Springer-Praxis, 2000.
Jack Cohen and Ian Stewart	*What Does a Martian Look Like? The Science of Extraterrestrial Life.* Hoboken, NJ: John Wiley & Sons, 2002.
David Darling	*Life Everywhere: The Maverick Science of Astrobiology.* New York: Basic Books, 2001.
Brenda Denzler	*The Lure of the Edge: Scientific Passions, Religious Beliefs, and the Pursuit of UFOs.* Berkeley: University of California Press, 2001.
Steven J. Dick and James E. Strick	*The Living Universe: NASA and the Development of Astrobiology.* New Brunswick, NJ: Rutgers University Press, 2004.
Steven J. Dick, ed.	*Many Worlds: The New Universe, Extraterrestrial Life and the Theological Implications.* Philadelphia: Templeton Foundation, 2000.
Ronald D. Ekers, D. Kent Cullers, and John Billingham	*SETI 2020: A Roadmap for the Search for Extraterrestrial Intelligence.* SETI, 2002.
Timothy Ferris	*Life Beyond Earth.* New York: Simon & Schuster, 2000.
Donald Goldsmith and Tobias Owen	*The Search for Life in the Universe.* 3rd ed. Sausalito, CA: University Science Books, 2002.
Monica M. Grady	*Astrobiology.* Washington, DC: Smithsonian, 2001.
Steven M. Greer	*Disclosure: Military and Government Witnesses Reveal the Greatest Secrets in Modern History.* Crozer, VA: Crossing Point, 2001.
David Grinspoon	*Lonely Planets: The Natural Philosophy of Alien Life.* New York: Ecco, 2003.
Budd Hopkins and Carol Rainey	*Sight Unseen: Science, UFO Invisibility and Transgenic Beings.* New York: Atria, 2003.
David M. Jacobs, ed.	*UFOs and Abductions: Challenging the Borders of Knowledge.* Lawrence: University Press of Kansas, 2000.

David Koerner and Simon LeVay	*Here Be Dragons: The Scientific Quest for Extraterrestrial Life.* New York: Oxford University Press, 2000.
David Lamb	*The Search for Extraterrestrial Intelligence: A Philosophical Inquiry.* New York: Routledge, 2001.
James R. Lewis	*The Encyclopedic Sourcebook of UFO Religions.* Amherst, NY: Prometheus, 2003.
Brian S. McConnell	*Beyond Contact: A Guide to SETI and Communicating with Alien Civilizations.* Sebastopol, CA: O'Reilly, 2001
John F. Moffit	*Picturing Extraterrestrials: Alien Images in Modern Mass Culture.* Amherst, NY: Prometheus, 2003.
Susan J. Palmer	*Aliens Adored: Rael's UFO Religion.* New Brunswick, NJ: Rutgers University Press, 2004.
Christopher Partridge	*UFO Religions.* New York: Routledge, 2003.
Lynn Picknett	*The Mammoth Book of UFOs.* New York: Carroll & Graf, 2001.
Seth Shostak and Alex Barnett	*Cosmic Company: The Search for Life in the Universe.* New York: Cambridge University Press, 2003.
Gloria Skurzynski	*Are We Alone? Scientists Search for Life in Space.* Washington, DC: National Geographic Society, 2004.
P. Ulmschneider	*Intelligent Life in the Universe: From Common Origins to the Future of Humanity.* New York: Springer, 2003.
Peter D. Ward and Donald Brownlee	*Rare Earth: Why Complex Life Is Uncommon in the Universe.* New York: Copernicus, 2000.
Steven Webb	*Where Is Everybody? Fifty Solutions to the Fermi Paradox and the Problem of Extraterrestrial Life.* New York: Copernicus, 2002.

Periodicals

Joel Achenbach and Peter Essick	"Life Beyond Earth," *National Geographic*, January 2000.
Erik Baard	"In Search of Planets and Life," *Ad Astra*, January/February/March 2004.
Jack Cohen and Ian Stewart	"Where Are the Dolphins?" *Nature*, February 2, 2001.
J. Deardorff, B. Haisch, B. Maccabee, and H.E. Puthoff	"Inflation Theory Implications for Extraterrestrial Visitation," *Journal of the British Interplanetary Society*, no. 1, 2005.
Cynthia Fox	"The Search for Extraterrestrial Life," *Life*, March 2000.
Frederick Golden	"Will We Meet E.T.?" *Time*, April 10, 2000.
Donald Goldsmith	"Bolts from Beyond," *Natural History*, September 2003.
Monica M. Grady	"Astrobiology: The Search for Life Beyond Earth," *Geology Today*, May/June 2003.
David Grinspoon	"SETI and the Science Wars," *Astronomy*, May 2000.

Michio Kaku	"Who Will Inherit the Universe?" *Astronomy*, February 2002.
Andrew J. LePage	"Where Could They Hide?" *Scientific American*, July 2000.
Samuel McCracken	"Close Encounters of the Harvard Kind," *Commentary*, March 2000.
Michael A.G. Michaud	"Ten Decisions That Could Shake the World," *Space Policy*, May 2003.
Steve Nadis	"Look Who's Talking," *New Scientist*, July 12, 2003.
Jill Neimark	"Are Recovered Memories Real?" *Discover*, August 2004.
Steven Novella	"UFOs: The Psychocultural Hypothesis," *New England Journal of Skepticism*, Fall 2000.
Robert L. Park	"Welcome to Planet Earth," *Sciences*, May/June 2000.
Jay W. Richards and Guillermo Gonzalez	"Are We Alone?" *American Spectator*, May 2004.
Christopher Rose and Gregory Wright	"Inscribed Matter as an Energy-Efficient Means of Communication with an Extraterrestrial Civilization," *Nature*, September 2, 2004.
Lynn Rothchild	"Life in Extreme Environments," *Ad Astra*, January/February 2002.
Oliver Sacks	"Anybody Out There?" *Natural History*, November 2002.
Michael Shermer	"Shermer's Last Law," *Scientific American*, January 2002.
Seth Shostak	"Listening for a Whisper," *Astronomy*, September 2004.
Laurence Squeri	"When ET Calls: SETI Is Ready," *Journal of Popular Culture*, no. 3, 2004.
Sally Stephens	"Listening for E.T." *Astronomy*, December 2001.
Michael Sturma	"Alien Abductions," *History Today*, January 2000.
Woodruff T. Sullivan III	"Astrobiology: Message in a Bottle," *Nature*, September 2, 2004.
Jill Tarter	"SETI and the Religions of Extraterrestrials," *Free Inquiry*, Summer 2000.
John Whitfield	"Exobiology: It's Life . . . Isn't It?" *Nature*, July 15, 2004.
Jim Wilson	"Roswell Declassified," *Popular Mechanics*, June 2003.
T.L. Wilson	"The Search for Extraterrestrial Intelligence," *Nature*, February 22, 2001.

Video and DVD

Timothy Ferris — *Life Beyond Earth*, PBS Home Video, 2001. A documentary about the scientific search for life in the universe featuring beautiful space photos and special effects.

Peter Jennings — "Seeing Is Believing," *ABC News*, February 24, 2005. A television journalist's investigation of current opinions about UFOs.

PBS — "Mars, Dead or Alive," *NOVA*, PBS Home Video, 2004. A documentary about what science is discovering about Mars.

INDEX